Praise for *The Gluten-Free Edge*

"*The Gluten-Free Edge* is an excellent book for anyone who wants to cook gluten-free recipes and learn more about the gluten-free lifestyle. Anyone who wants to improve their health will benefit from this book. I highly recommend that you read *The Gluten-Free Edge*."

—Scott Adams, founder, *www.GlutenFreeMall.com*

"Of all the lifestyle management issues addressed in our integrative medical clinic, the elimination of gluten-containing foods is the most difficult. Gluten seems to appear everywhere on the American culinary scene, and creating a tasteful and satisfying nutritional program without it can be a frustrating experience. Many patients give up, claiming they just can't figure it out. Fortunately, *The Gluten-Free Edge* is a comprehensive and thoroughly usable presentation of a complicated and increasingly important subject."

—Allan E. Sosin, MD, founder and medical director of the Institute for Progressive Medicine and the National Health Federation's Physician of the Year in 2000

"Gini has done an excellent job of pulling together nutritious and tasty recipes in *The Gluten-Free Edge*. The book also contains an excellent overview of gluten-free tips and tricks that give beginners the information that they need. We're happy to see this project complete. Great job!"

—GlutenFreeClub.com

The Gluten-Free EDGE

Get Skinny the Gluten-Free Way!

Gini Warner, MA and **Chef Ross Harris**

Foreword by **Dr. Peter Green, MD,** Director of the Celiac Disease Center at Columbia University

Aadamsmedia
Avon, Massachusetts

To Carly, Amanda, Sidney, Ken, Lee, June, Bonnie, Millie, Bernie, Blanche, and Henry.

Published by
Adams Media, a division of F+W Media, Inc.
57 Littlefield Street, Avon, MA 02322. U.S.A.
www.adamsmedia.com

ISBN 10: 1-4405-1183-7
ISBN 13: 978-1-4405-1183-7
eISBN 10: 1-4405-1260-4
eISBN 13: 978-1-4405-1260-5

Printed in the United States of America.

10 9 8 7 6 5 4 3 2 1

Library of Congress Cataloging-in-Publication Data
is available from the publisher.

Contains a limited number of recipes previously published in *The Everything® Gluten-Free Cookbook* by Rick Marx and Nancy Maar, copyright © 2006 by F+W Media, Inc., ISBN 10: 1-59337-394-5, ISBN 13: 978-1-59337-394-8.

The information in this book should not be used for diagnosing or treating any health problem. Not all diet and exercise plans suit everyone. You should always consult a trained medical professional before starting a diet, taking any form of medication, or embarking on any fitness or weight-training program. The author and publisher disclaim any liability arising directly or indirectly from the use of this book.

Many of the designations used by manufacturers and sellers to distinguish their product are claimed as trademarks. Where those designations appear in this book and Adams Media was aware of a trademark claim, the designations have been printed with initial capital letters.

Interior photos by Bryan Ramsay, except as noted:
Blueberry Pancakes © Robyn Mackenzie, Panna Cotta © John Janssen,
Tomato Basil Soup © kivoart

This book is available at quantity discounts for bulk purchases.
For information, please call 1-800-289-0963.

ACKNOWLEDGMENTS

I spent nearly fifteen years trying to figure out what was causing all of the symptoms and discomfort that I was experiencing. One of the most enlightening moments of my life was when I made the connection between gluten and my health problems. Another pleasant surprise was when I met Chef Ross, who was eager to create gourmet gluten-free meals. I want to thank him for all of his support and creativity in working with me to write *The Gluten-Free Edge*. I would also like to recognize my clients, who were so enthusiastic about trying a gluten-free lifestyle. The improvement in their health problems and the significant weight loss that they achieved was truly an inspiration. I would like to thank Dr. Peter Green for all of his great work in helping so many people to solve the mystery of the root cause of their medical problems.

—*Gini Warner, Nutritionist*

I want to pay tribute to Gini Warner for teaching me about gluten intolerance. I have always happily prepared gluttonous feasts for myself and my clients, but Gini has inspired me to dramatically change my menu selections. As a result, my health and energy levels have improved noticeably. The most unexpected part is how happy my clients are with my new gluten-free recipe selections. I want to thank my friends and clients for their encouragement and excitement over the creation of this book.

—*Chef Ross Harris*

TABLE OF CONTENTS

FOREWORD

Gini Warner and Ross Harris's book, *The Gluten-Free Edge*, is a wonderful compilation of fabulous recipes for managing a delicious gluten-free lifestyle. This cookbook offers both adults and children a wonderful way to enjoy a gluten-free diet.

People who suffer from gluten intolerance are unable to process the gluten that exists in their foods. *Gluten* is the term for the storage protein of wheat. There are similar proteins, to which people with celiac disease react, found in rye and barley. As a result, the latter two grains are included in the grains to be avoided when an individual is on a gluten-free diet. All other grains are tolerated by over 99 percent of those with celiac disease. Gluten intolerance can be traced to the fact that the human digestive system does not break down gluten as thoroughly as other proteins, leaving large amino acid fragments. In genetically predisposed people, these fragments trigger an inflammatory response in the small intestine that causes villous atrophy. This mechanism is more fully described in the book I coauthored, *Celiac Disease: A Hidden Epidemic*.

Gluten intolerance manifests in several forms, as gluten sensitive enteropathy, or celiac disease; dermatitis herpetiformis, or DH; or gluten intolerance without celiac disease. Gluten sensitive enteropathy, or celiac disease, is a lifelong, unique autoimmune illness. It occurs in about 1 percent of the population, worldwide. There is little knowledge among physicians about the subtle clinical presentations, use of serologic testing, and long-term management. In addition to a gluten-free diet, those with celiac disease require advice and counseling about nutritious and varied substitutes for gluten (similar to the ingredients described in this book), assessment and monitoring of their health and nutrition status, and good medical follow-up for their disease, as those with celiac disease have an increased burden of disease compared to the general population. Patients in the United States often get no or inadequate medical follow-up. This compares dramatically with the health-care systems in most European countries, where celiac disease is regarded as a common and important condition. It is only with good, ongoing medical care, and great attention to a varied and nutritious diet, that an adequate quality of life can be maintained. Many people worldwide have adopted a gluten-free diet. For those with celiac disease, this diet can be lifesaving, while others simply find that the relief from gastrointestinal or neurological symptoms makes their life much more comfortable.

The Celiac Disease Center at Columbia University provides comprehensive medical care for adults and pediatric patients with celiac disease, including nutrition and attention to the multiple associated conditions that occur in celiac disease. The center is involved in the care of thousands of patients with celiac disease and gluten intolerance, providing better access to proper testing, diagnosis, treatment, and follow-up care.

All of the center's research is directed toward celiac disease and reflects the nature of celiac disease as a multisystem disease including cardiovascular disease, cancer, thyroid disease, infertility, and psychiatric and behavior problems in childhood. Additional information is available online at *www.celiacdiseasecenter.org*.

Celiac disease and gluten intolerance are great examples of why we need to know what we are eating. This is something that is increasingly difficult in this day and age where food is often grown far from where we live, and is made more complicated with the prevalence of processed foods, fast foods, and food additives. *The Gluten-Free Edge* helps in that Gini and Ross not only provide copious amounts of information about available gluten-free ingredients, but also provide recipes that allow everyone to make gluten-free homemade meals from scratch.

There is no doubt that resources such as this book are an important adjunct to any household that is attempting to be gluten-free. I congratulate Gini and Ross on their superb efforts. Read the book and enjoy the delicious gluten-free recipes!

Peter H.R. Green, MD
Professor of Clinical Medicine
Columbia University Medical Center
Director, Celiac Disease Center at Columbia University Medical Center
www.celiacdiseasecenter.org

INTRODUCTION

Have you tried to lose weight, but been unsuccessful? Have you lost weight, and then gained it all back once you stopped following a specific diet? You might be surprised to find that the likely culprit is a diet full of gluten-containing processed foods.

In 2001, the *American Journal of Gastroenterology* published a study showing that 39 percent of the nearly 3 million Americans with celiac disease are overweight at diagnosis, and a full 30 percent are obese. Many of these people lose their extra weight for good once they stop eating gluten-filled processed foods. You may already know that gluten is dangerous for people who have celiac disease or gluten intolerance, but you don't have to have these conditions to reap the weight-loss benefits of a gluten-free diet. *The Gluten-Free Edge* gives you everything you need to successfully—and safely—reach your weight-loss goals.

What Is Gluten?

The simple answer is that gluten is a complex protein found in wheat, barley, rye, and contaminated oats (oats that were processed in a facility that processes gluten-containing foods) that keeps the small intestine from properly absorbing the nutrients that you take in. Gluten is also found in a wide variety of other processed foods and is used as a binder and thickener.

Before we go any further, it is important for you to understand that wheat, barley, and rye are actually genetically derived from wild grasses. Humans, developing as hunters and gatherers, developed these grains in order to provide themselves with a quick source of food and calories. This made it easier for them to obtain food without hunting, as well as to guard against food shortage. However, many Americans have a certain gene that targets gluten as a foreign protein that affects the immune system. The human immune system isn't built to recognize or digest the gluten, which contains a toxic chain of amino acids called *gliadin*. Gliadin is the protein that gives many people, with and without celiac disease, the most trouble in the small intestine. The small intestine is lined with *villi*, small projections that increase the surface area of the intestine and help with nutrient absorption. Gliadin damages these villi, which can result in your body being unable to absorb nutrients that it needs to stay healthy, slowing down your metabolism and keeping you from losing weight.

Most breads, pastas, cereals, and desserts contain gluten, and eating these carbohydrates can make you feel tired and sluggish and can result in weight gain. Research also indicates that many of these gluten-containing foods are also very high in fat and refined sugar. Eating foods high in refined sugar can cause elevated insulin levels, which often induce cravings for more gluten-filled, processed foods. These foods also encourage your body to produce endorphins, chemicals that make you feel great. This results in a vicious cycle of overeating and weight gain. If you cut the offending, gluten-filled processed foods out of your diet and replace them with gluten-free meals that you make yourself, you'll reduce your cravings for desserts and carbohydrate-rich processed foods, which will make it much easier to take off those extra pounds. After all, it's much easier to turn something down if your mouth isn't watering at just the thought of it.

Feel Better, Live Better

While going gluten-free may sound difficult, the benefits truly are well worth it in the long run—and we're proof of that. I have been living a gluten-free lifestyle for years now due to my history of gluten intolerance and I recommend that my clients follow suit—whether they are having health problems related to gluten intolerance or just want to clean up their diet. My coauthor, Chef Ross Harris, has completely eliminated gluten from his professional recipes and his personal diet. He now is at his ideal body weight and his energy levels have shot through the roof.

But just because you're cutting gluten out of your diet doesn't mean that you have to cut out taste. Chef Harris's experience with the gluten-free lifestyle has influenced his cooking over the years and he's developed a variety of recipes that make it easy to go gluten-free without giving up delicious, gourmet meals. The tasty, creative, healthy recipes that you'll find inside will give you the edge you need to get the weight-loss results you crave. Many people report feeling an enormous increase in energy and clarity of mind after cutting gluten out of their diets; they are able to work harder and exercise more rigorously, are more inclined to make healthier food choices, and are able to lose weight that they thought they would never be able to lose. This can happen for you too—if you're ready to make the commitment. To jump-start your new lifestyle, you'll find tips on going gluten-free in Part 1, recipes in Part 2, and a seven-day weight-loss plan in Part 3 that makes it easy to cut gluten-filled foods out of your daily diet and get you on the right track to a healthy weight. Good luck, and enjoy!

Going Gluten-Free

Going gluten-free isn't easy, but it's important to eliminate these gluten-containing, processed foods if you are trying to lose weight. Most people report that staying on track can be difficult in the beginning—after all, it's hard to say "no" to an offer from a group of friends to go out for pizza—but to be successful you just have to commit to and educate yourself about the gluten-free lifestyle. To help make the transition easier, in this part you'll find:

- A list of foods to avoid (including foods that may contain hidden gluten)
- A list of foods that are gluten-free
- Info about the rules for gluten-free labeling and what to watch out for on food labels
- Tips for cooking at home and for successfully dining out
- Tips for staying gluten-free while traveling

Learning what you need to do to go gluten-free can seem confusing at first, but reading labels and eating more foods that are in their natural state will help you become more familiar with the lifestyle. If you start slowly and gradually eliminate gluten-filled foods from your diet, with time, creativity, and patience, you will find many enjoyable, delicious foods (many in the recipe section later on in the book) that are entirely gluten-free.

What Should I Avoid?

The question many of my clients ask when we first discuss a gluten-free diet is, "What do I have to give up?" Fortunately, you can actually eat more foods than you may think. We'll discuss those foods later on, but let's first take a look at the products and foods you should stay away from.

Wheat, Barley, Rye, and Contaminated Oats

You know that a gluten-free diet requires you to give up wheat, barley, and rye, but sometimes these grains are hidden in various foods. Barley is used in many food products, including bread, soups, whiskey, and beer. It's also often combined with wheat flour in recipes for many baked goods and can be found in syrups and some flavorings that are added to foods. It is often found in instant coffee and coffee substitutes. Rye is found in pumpernickel bread and in certain alcoholic beverages, such as some brands of vodka and whiskey.

Watch out for products that contain the following:

- **Semolina:** The majority of pasta available at grocery stores is made out of semolina wheat flour. Couscous, which looks similar to rice, is actually made of semolina flour and is therefore classified as a type of pasta.
- **Durum:** Many of the finest pastas will say "made from durum semolina." Durum is the hardest type of wheat.
- **Orzo:** Very small pasta that is made from semolina.
- **Farina:** This grain is a type of semolina. It is used in many hot cereals.
- **Graham flour:** This is unbleached whole wheat flour that is used in many pie crusts.
- **Bulgur:** A type of whole wheat commonly found in cereals, soups, stuffings, and bread.
- **Kamut:** A type of wheat often found in natural foods that are sold in specialty markets. It is considered to be a bit healthier than most wheat flours.
- **Seitan:** A wheat-based product. Often used as a meat substitute in vegetarian recipes.
- **Spelt (a form of wheat):** Spelt is often used in breads and pastas and has more protein than other types of wheat.
- **Triticale:** Triticale is a hybrid grain produced by crossbreeding wheat and rye. It is found in some breakfast cereals.
- **Oats:** This grain is okay for most people on a gluten-free diet. Even people with celiac seem to tolerate oats, but some people can have a reaction. It is best to buy oats that are labeled gluten-free.

Foods to Avoid

There are many foods, beverages, and nonfood products that contain gluten so it is important that you check the ingredients and read the package labels completely to see if your foods have been processed along with wheat. In addition, a product might be gluten-free now, but the manufacturer could change the ingredients at any time. Therefore, it is imperative to read labels every time you shop. If you are still unsure, call the product manufacturer. Avoid the following foods if they are not labeled as being gluten-free, if you see gluten-containing ingredients listed on the label, or if they might be cross-contaminated.

- **Breads:** All white, wheat, rye, and sourdough breads are made with gluten. Gluten firms up when it's cooked, which helps to maintain the shape of bread and gives bread its chewy texture.
- **Cakes and pies:** Unless labeled gluten-free, cakes and pies are usually made with gluten-containing flour.
- **Candy:** Pure chocolate and cocoa have no gluten, and many chocolate-based candy bars are gluten-free. Several candy companies, like See's, offer a selection of gluten-free chocolate treats. Avoid candy bars with a "cookie" component to them. The cookie in the candy is often made with gluten-containing flour. Several brands of chewing gum are safe, such as Wrigley's and Bubble Yum.
- **Luncheon meats:** If you buy sliced meat at your deli counter, ask them to carefully clean the slicer before slicing your meat to avoid cross-contamination.
- **Cereals:** Most are high in gluten unless made with only gluten-free grains.
- **Cookies**
- **Crackers**
- **Croutons**
- **Enhanced rice or flavored rice dishes**
- **Frozen vegetables with sauce packets:** The sauce in the packets is made with thickeners that often contain flour.
- **Gravy, both packaged and bottled:** Many gravies begin with a roux base, which consists of butter and flour for thickening.
- **Imitation bacon bits:** May contain gluten, which is often found in additives and preservatives.
- **Imitation meat or seafood**
- **Pasta**
- **Self-basting poultry**
- **Salad dressings:** Several brands of salad dressings are gluten-free, such as Annie's Naturals and Organicville, but some manufacturers and many restaurants may add gluten for thickening.

- **Sauces and marinades (including soy sauce):** Some soy sauces are gluten-free, but many are not. It is best to avoid all premade marinades in restaurants including teriyaki sauce.
- **Soups:** Canned and boxed soups use wheat as a thickener. Do not buy any commercial bouillon cubes or soup stock without reading the label. Most restaurants use gluten-containing ingredients in their soup base. Make sure to inquire before ordering soup.

In addition, there are many beverages that may contain gluten, including cocoa mixes, root beer, chocolate drinks, and various beverage mixes.

Hidden Gluten

There are many foods, beverages, and nonfood products that contain hidden gluten. It may not be obvious when reading a label that a food or beverage contains gluten, because a product can be labeled gluten-free but still contain barley, malt, or rye. The following is a list of places where gluten may be hiding:

- **Baking powder**
- **Beer: lager, stout, and ale**
- **Bouillon cubes and powder**
- **Cheese:** Most cheese is naturally gluten-free, but it could become contaminated during manufacturing. It is best to buy cheese that is packaged and labeled gluten-free.
- **Chili powder**
- **Flavored coffees**
- **Fried foods:** Many fried foods have gluten in the batter. In addition, they may become cross-contaminated if cooked in a pan that was previously used to cook food containing gluten.
- **Dried fruits:** Some companies dust dried fruit with flour, so read labels carefully.
- **Foods sold in bins:** Most of these foods contain gluten. The gluten could come from a previous gluten-containing food that was in the same bin last week.

- **French fries:** Avoid most frozen fries and French fries cooked in a restaurants, due to cross-contamination.
- **Imitation seafood:** The fillers might contain wheat starch.
- **Lemonade:** Commercial lemonade often contains malt and/or barley.
- **Modified food starch:** If the source of the modified food starch is wheat starch, it is not safe. In the United States, if you see the word *starch* on the label it means cornstarch, which is safe.
- **Nuts:** Read the small print on packages. Often nuts are processed in a plant that processes wheat. Therefore, there might be cross-contamination.
- **Salad dressing and mayonnaise:** Most are safe, but watch out for barley malt as an ingredient in salad dressing. The dressing might say "gluten-free," but it could contain barley malt.
- **Seasoning mixes**
- **White pepper**
- **Yogurt (many reduced-fat and flavored varieties)**

Nonfood Products

Many nonfood products that you come in contact with every day may contain gluten. Watch out for cross-contamination, which can result anywhere ingredients can come together. If you have celiac disease these products can be dangerous but even if you don't have celiac disease, it can be helpful to look into the following products to ensure you remain gluten-free.

Vitamin and mineral supplements: Some brands may be labeled "wheat-free" but this does not mean that they are definitely gluten free. Check with the manufacturer before taking any nutritional supplements.

Medication: It may seem surprising, but medications often contain gluten. Many manufacturers will dust pills with flour and may put gluten in the oil that is inside of the pill. In fact, the majority of prescription medications use either a corn base or a wheat base. If your pharmacist is not sure, you should call the manufacturer to be safe. You can also ensure that you remain gluten-free by filling your prescription from a pharmacy (or online provider) that offers gluten-free alternatives. Check out *www.glutenfreedrugs.com* for more info.

Skin care products or cosmetics: Skin care products or cosmetics are only concerning if they come into contact with your mouth and you consume gluten.

I recommend using gluten-free lipstick and lip balms to avoid consuming them while eating; check with the manufacturer before using lipstick. Some gluten-free brands include Burt's Bees and Neutrogena. In addition, toothpaste and mouthwash may also be swallowed accidentally. Most popular brands, including Crest and Colgate, are gluten-free.

What *Can* I Eat?

The word *diet* technically implies deprivation or some sort of sacrifice, but when you follow a gluten-free diet you will actually be getting much more nutritional value in the foods you eat. By enjoying the rich and delicious recipes included in this book and using the following list of gluten-free foods, you will be able to make a smooth transition to a healthy lifestyle. The key is to choose as many whole foods as you can, such as fruits, vegetables, nuts, beans, and unprocessed meats.

The variety of gluten-free foods include the following:

- **Fresh meats, fish, and poultry:** Avoid bacon and sausage unless they are labeled gluten-free because they might contain gluten fillers. Also avoid meats that are breaded, batter-coated, marinated, or preseasoned, as these coatings and marinades may contain gluten.
- **Dairy products:** The majority of dairy products are gluten-free, but you should avoid cheeses that are sliced in the store because they may be contaminated with gluten. It is best to stick with cheeses that are labeled gluten-free.
- **Fruits:** All fresh fruit, frozen whole fruits with no additives, and fruit juice (100 percent fruit).
- **Nuts and seeds (unsalted, raw):** All nuts in their pure form are safe as long as they are not coated, but prepacked trail mixes might contain gluten. Seeds and most nut butters are safe. Read labels to be sure.
- **Vegetables:** All fresh vegetables, all frozen vegetables (with no additives, breading, or sauces), all fresh and canned beans, olives, potatoes (all varieties), and lentils.
- **Rice:** Stay away from enriched, flavored, or seasoned versions.
- **Potatoes:** Fresh potatoes are a good choice and, in fact, potato flour and potato starch are used to thicken many gluten-free foods.
- **Rice noodles**

- **Beans and lentils**
- **Meats, eggs, and soy foods:** All fresh lean meats, poultry with no breading or additives, eggs (check the labels on all egg substitutes for gluten-containing ingredients), soybeans (including edamame), tofu, soy milk (plain, unsweetened), soy mayonnaise, and soy butter.
- **Vinegars (except malt vinegar and grain vinegar):** Vinegars, such as red wine vinegar, apple cider vinegar, and balsamic vinegar also do not contain gluten because they do not come from a gluten-containing grain.
- **Distilled liquors, ciders, and spirits**
- **Arrowroot:** Arrowroot is a plant that is found in a rainforest-type climate. This particular starch is easy to digest and is great for thickening soup and gravy in gluten-free cooking.
- **Flours:** Coconut flour, carob flour, chestnut flour, garbanzo bean flour, soy flour, and potato flour are all gluten-free ingredients.
- **Spices:** Only buy spices in their pure form and make sure they are fresh. Many specialty markets sell a variety of gluten-free spices.
- **Herbs:** The best ones are fresh. Dried herbs can be subject to cross-contamination but are usually safe.
- **Coffee and tea:** Natural coffees and teas are gluten-free, but instant, decaffeinated, and flavored versions may contain gluten. Avoid drinking coffee that is made by someone else. If they used their coffee maker for gluten-containing coffee, there may be cross-contamination.
- **Seafood:** All fresh seafood in its natural state is gluten-free, as is all frozen seafood that doesn't include additives, sauces, or marinades.
- **Gluten-free breads, cereals, pasta, and crackers:** Read labels carefully and choose brands made without gluten-containing grains. Some brands include Joan's GF Great Bakes, Inc., and Arrowhead Mills GF cereals.

Your Complete Shopping List

When you first start going gluten-free it might seem easier to buy ready-made products at the supermarket than it is to cook and bake gluten-free foods. This is a good first step as long as you focus on unprocessed foods that are naturally gluten free, but you should cook or bake from scratch as often as you possibly can. Not only will it save you money, but you'll have no doubt as to whether or not the food you're eating is gluten-free. Also, just because these processed foods are labeled gluten-free doesn't mean that they are necessarily healthy; keep in mind that many processed foods are high in fat. When you cook at home as opposed to buying your food already prepared you cut out much of the fat and added sugar and many calories, and you'll begin to see your desired weight-loss results much more quickly.

The following shopping list will make it easier for you to select the wide variety of gluten-free foods that are available to you. You can eat any of the fresh foods in the preceding list, but the items on the list that follows will point you in the right direction for various premade foods. This is not a complete list of gluten-free foods, but when you're just starting out on a gluten-free diet, it helps to have a basic list of brands that you can keep handy. To find out if your grocery store or supermarket carries additional gluten-free products, check with the customer service desk; many grocery stores and supermarkets are now providing complete lists of gluten-free products available in their store. Keep in mind though, you still need to check the labels on everything you buy—especially if you're buying processed foods. Check your grocery store for the following brands:

PASTAS

- Bio Nature pasta
- Lundberg (rice and chips as well as pastas)
- De Boles Pasta
- Tinkyada (rice pasta)

CANNED PRODUCTS

- American Tuna Pole wild caught albacore—no salt added
- Amy's Organic Chili

CEREALS

- Blueberry Fields granola cascade crunch
- Enjoy Life (manufacturer of cereal, cereal bars, cookies, and chocolates)
- Rice Chex cereal
- Corn Chex cereal

CONDIMENTS AND SEASONINGS

- Amy's salsa
- Annie's Naturals salad dressings
- Bionaturea fruit spread
- Bragg's organic sprinkle seasoning
- MaraNatha organic peanut butter
- Nasoya (gluten-free mayonnaise)
- Organicville dressing
- San-J Tamari Soy Sauce
- Spectrum light canola mayo
- Vivi's sauces

NONDAIRY BEVERAGES AND PRODUCTS

- Soy Dream soy milk
- Pacific Almond Milk
- Living Harvest hemp milk

EXTRAS

- Think Thin (gluten-free protein bars)
- Barkat Brown Rice Pizza Crust
- Bob's Red Mill oats, steel cut
- Bob's Red Mill garbanzo/fava flour
- Lundberg brown rice couscous
- Yummy Earth organic candy drops

If you are in doubt about any product, be sure to check with the manufacturer.

Gluten-Free Labeling

If you're buying your food at the supermarket, you may expect items to alert you as to whether or not they contain gluten. Unfortunately, there is currently no legislation in the United States that provides a standard for gluten-free labeling. However, the Federal Drug Administration (FDA) does recognize the need to warn people if a product contains any of the eight food allergens. In 2006 the FDA introduced food allergen labeling that warns consumers if a product contains one of the eight major allergens: milk, egg, wheat, soy, peanut, tree nuts, fish, and crustacean shellfish. This labeling makes it easy for you to identify whether a product contains gluten from wheat. However, a product could contain gluten from barley, contaminated oats, rye, or cross-contamination, which companies are not currently required to identify.

The reality is that you should read labels on every product you purchase if you are on a gluten-free diet. This is because companies can change their ingredients. A product that was once gluten-free could suddenly contain gluten if the ingredient list was modified or changed. In addition, a product may be labeled gluten-free and still contain ingredients that have gluten. A study done by Reuters found that some grains that are supposed to be naturally gluten-free can be cross-contaminated if they are grown or processed near other grains that do contain gluten.

Fortunately there are many U.S. companies that have dedicated themselves to making gluten-free products, and these products often say "gluten-free" on the label. Many gluten-free products are available in the organic or natural food sections of most mainstream grocery stores. You can also order gluten-free foods and get product information online.

Products That Are Gluten-Free

In addition, the following grains are naturally gluten-free, and they are used in many gluten-free recipes. Read labels carefully or check with the manufacturer to verify that these are processed in a gluten-free facility before consuming them.

- **Amaranth:** This cream-colored flour has a nutty and sweet taste. It is great for making a thick crust and browns quickly. It is also perfect for thickening sauces and gravies and making pancakes, muffins, and pizza dough. You can use amaranth flour to replace up to ¼ of the total flour in any recipe calling for all-purpose gluten-free flour. It is best used in recipes that do not contain a lot of liquids.
- **Buckwheat:** You may think that buckwheat is a grain because of its name, but buckwheat is actually a fruit. It is high in fiber and B vitamins, which is a plus for people with celiac disease. Buckwheat is one of the few commercially grown crops that does not use chemicals.
- **Rice:** Pure rice is naturally gluten-free. Flavored, enriched and seasoned rice may contain gluten, so read labels carefully.
- **Corn:** Flour made from corn makes a great substitute for gluten-containing flours.
- **Millet:** Rich in nutrients and great to cook with. Read labels carefully to be sure it has been processed in a gluten-free facility.
- **Quinoa:** This grain provides an excellent source of protein and has a rich flavor.

Gluten-Free Cooking at Home

Many people who are just getting started on a gluten-free diet get caught up in eating a lot of gluten-free bread, pasta, baked goods, and processed foods, but cooking with gluten-free ingredients is easy and the food tastes great. When you eliminate these processed foods from many of your meals, you'll quickly notice that the flavors of natural ingredients are more distinct and actually work to enhance each other's flavors. You'll truly be able to taste the flavors of the foods that you're cooking once the additives and preservatives found in processed foods are taken out of the picture.

It is important for you to know what gluten does to food before you attempt to cook without it. Gluten gives food a lot of elasticity and a sticky consistency, which is why dough has a stretchy, gluey feeling about it. If you've ever seen a hand-tossed pizza thrown to stretch it into shape, you've seen gluten in action. How much water is added to the dish and how much the dough is mixed or kneaded has a noticeable effect on how flexible the dough becomes. The water makes the dough lighter when baked and the act of kneading dough causes the gluten in it to form into strands. This is why, once yeast is added, dough rises; as the yeast produces gas, the gas is trapped by sheets of gluten strands.

All of the recipes in this book incorporate various gluten substitutes, which ensures that your food tastes great even with the gluten removed. For example, when thickening sauces, soups, and gravies, you can use cornstarch, potato starch, arrowroot, tapioca, or garbanzo flour in place of wheat flour. For baked products, you can substitute rice, potato, corn, soy, or a blend of these or other gluten-free flours. Garbanzo flour is also an excellent choice. It is high in protein and low in fat. Keep in mind that, when you're cooking with these gluten-free substitutes, you may need to adjust measurements and the other ingredients in recipes to get the same flavor.

Some additional substitutions include the following:

Product Containing Gluten	Gluten-Free Substitute
Semolina or durum (wheat) pasta	Rice or corn pasta
Soy sauce	Wheat-free tamari
Seitan (wheat meat)	Baked tofu
Bulgur	Quinoa
Couscous	Quinoa or millet
Flour tortillas	Corn tortillas

You'll notice that many of the recipes in Part 2 use gluten-free flours. These can be substituted on a one-to-one ratio for wheat flour. There are many commercial brands available. Make sure to read the labels and select the ones lowest in fat and sugar. You can also use gluten-free oats in your cooking. In the past, oats were not seen as a safe, gluten-free alternative because when oats are handled by the same equipment and grown in the same fields as wheat, cross-contamination is likely. Now, many grain growers have started using separate fields and equipment when handling products that are intended to be gluten-free. You can now even find vendors specializing in gluten-free oats.

Avoid Cross-Contamination

Many people worry about contamination in the kitchen, but you can curb this by using pots and pans that are dedicated to gluten-free cooking. Designate a cutting board and butter dish to be used for gluten-free foods only and clean toaster ovens and microwaves carefully after they've been used for gluten-containing foods. Make sure your food prep surfaces, utensils, mixer, and pans are free of any kind of gluten residue. Buy a new toaster and use it only for gluten-free toasting. In addition, you may want to buy a hand blender and a food processor with medium-large capacity if you don't have those already. These appliances are essential in preparing and combining unprocessed ingredients. The following kitchen products will also be helpful in preparing your gluten-free meals:

- **Eight-inch chef's knife:** The most versatile cooking knife
- **Five-inch Santoku knife:** For preparation of vegetables and fruits
- **Three-inch paring knife:** Good for peeling vegetables and fruit
- **A few large, medium, and small mixing bowls**
- **Kitchen shears:** A scissor used for cutting vegetables and shellfish
- **A set of wooden kitchen tools:** spatula, fork, spoons
- **A set of silicone spatulas:** good for mixing and spreading
- **One medium and one small whisk**
- **Pyrex bakeware including pans and bowls:** Used for baking entrées and desserts
- **Nonstick baking sheets**
- **Nonstick cupcake pans:** Used for breakfast recipes and desserts
- **Small, medium, and large sauté pans**
- **Small, medium, and large saucepans**
- **A zester/grater:** For zesting fruit and grating spices

Party Planning

It's especially important to avoid cross-contaminating gluten-free foods with gluten when you're hosting other people at your home. If you are planning a barbecue for friends and family, check labels to make sure all condiments are gluten-free and try to grill the gluten-free food first, when the grates are clean. It is helpful to reserve a section of the grates just for the gluten-free food (be sure nothing with gluten drips onto it). If this is not possible, grill the gluten-free food on aluminum foil or in packets that will keep it off the grill surface. If you have people bringing dishes to a gathering at your home, be sure to label gluten-free foods to ensure that you—and your guests—know exactly what you're eating.

Dining Out Gluten-Free

When you're dining out, it's important to watch out for hidden gluten in sauces or cooking methods. However, this doesn't mean that you can't leave your house just because you're living a gluten-free lifestyle. Instead you just need to make some basic changes in what you eat and how your food is prepared. Meals eaten away from home need to be planned, and your lifestyle explained to anyone who cooks for you. You still want to live a full life, but you need to be in control of food preparation both at home and when eating out. Fortunately, with just a few precautions, you can eat almost anywhere.

Start by going to a restaurant with a small amount of food in your stomach. Don't go hungry, because the hungrier you are the more likely it is that you will rush into ordering and end up eating a gluten-filled meal. Bring some freshly cut raw carrots or rice crackers to snack on while everyone else is eating the bread. If you don't have any of these with you, ask the waiter to bring you some of those green olives that they have at the bar for you to eat while you're waiting for the meal to be served.

It's important to focus on clear communication with your waiters. Tell them that you cannot eat any gluten and ask them if they serve any gluten-free options. If they don't, you will be better off ordering your poultry, meat, and seafood grilled dry. Ask for vegetables cooked without sauce (olive oil and butter are okay). If your waiter brings you a salad with croutons on it when you asked for it without croutons, send it back and ask them to make it again. If you have gluten intolerance or celiac disease, don't remove the croutons yourself. There might be crouton crumbs remaining on the salad that can cause a reaction. In addition, salad dressings should always be ordered on the side, or better yet, always bring your own gluten-free dressing to be on the safe side. Feel free to ask your waiter the following questions:

- Are The Sauces, Gravies, Braised Dishes, Soups, Or Casseroles Thickened With Flour? If so, they may contain gluten. If the waiter is not sure, ask them not to put any sauce on the food.
- Is the pan-fried meat, poultry, or fish coated in flour before frying? Meat and fish seasonings can also contain wheat flour.
- Do the sauces contain soy sauce (most contain wheat), barbecue sauce, or Worcestershire sauce? (All are common sources of hidden gluten.)
- Has the food been marinated? Many marinades contain wheat flour or wheat.

When it comes time to place your order, ask your waiter to write it down. Many waiters try to remember all of the orders and they sometimes make mistakes.

Another way to keep yourself gluten-free and avoid hassle when dining out is to write the foods you can't eat down on a piece of paper that can be easily shown to a waiter or chef, or anyone preparing a meal for you. For example, I went to a restaurant and ordered fish, grilled dry. When it came to my table, it looked strange. I asked the waiter if it was powdered with flour prior to cooking. In their mind, it was still grilled dry, but the flour had gluten. I had to send it back and specifically ask them to cook the fish without the flour.

To make eating out easier, select restaurants that specialize gluten-free foods. Some restaurants will post their menu online so you can view it in advance or you can call the restaurant in advance to discuss your dietary needs and their menu options. Many restaurants will accommodate your needs and prepare foods without sauces.

Come Over for Dinner!

You may dread going over to someone else's house for dinner, especially if your host is unfamiliar with gluten-free foods, but take the time to explain your dietary restrictions to your family and friends. Oftentimes, they'll be interested to learn about your new gluten-free lifestyle. When dining at someone else's home, the easiest thing to do is to simply bring something that you can eat just in case the meal that is served is loaded with gluten or to give your host suggestions of foods that you can eat.

Getting Rid of Gluten

Now that you know what you should and shouldn't eat and the easiest ways to make going gluten-free work for you, you might be wondering when you'll start to see results. The timing is different for everyone. You want to consider the following factors:

- How long your body been exposed to gluten
- How careful you are about making sure you don't ingest any gluten
- How old you are, and what your overall diet looks like (The bodies of older adults take longer to remove gluten, and for everyone it's helpful to take good care of yourself and choose very healthy, nutrient-dense foods.)

It is important to have a clear understanding of the gluten-free diet and stick to it strictly. By choosing from the nutritious recipes in Part 2 and the variety of whole foods that are available to you, the results should occur quickly. Exercise on a regular basis and try your best to manage your stress levels. You will know when you're getting the gluten out of your system as you start to feel better.

Get Checked Out

If you feel markedly better as soon as you begin a gluten-free diet, there is a chance that you've been unknowingly suffering from celiac disease or non-celiac gluten intolerance. As we've discussed, people eat gluten so often because it exists in so many foods and gluten sensitivity, a separate disease that involves different organs than celiac disease, is very common. For many people, a traumatic event "turns on" the predisposition in the body, and they then begin to struggle with gluten intolerance. There are a wide range of symptoms and reactions that may indicate gluten sensitivity, such as:

- Malabsorption of nutrients
- Constant fatigue
- Frequent headaches
- Diarrhea
- Constipation
- Gas
- Bloating

- Thyroid problems
- Lactose intolerance
- Skin problems such as dermatitis herpetiformis (DH, or psoriasis)

These symptoms are related to gluten intolerance, but they may also indicate many other medical conditions. Professional medical advice should always be sought when trying to determine a cause.

Risk Factors

The following are risk factors associated with developing gluten intolerance. If you have any of these risk factors, discuss the possibility of gluten intolerance with your doctor or nutritionist:

- Microscopic colitis
- Family members with gluten sensitivities
- Inflammatory bowel disease (IBS)
- Chronic liver disease
- Dermatitis herpetiformis
- Diabetes mellitus, type 1
- Autoimmune thyroid disease
- Chronic fatigue
- Osteoporosis
- Iron deficiency
- Short stature in children

Overcoming Temptation

Whether you're trying to lose weight or are on a gluten-free diet for medical reasons, it's never easy to completely change your lifestyle and it's very common to be tempted to cheat. However, you can overcome the urge by thinking about why you want to cheat and the consequences of eating gluten-filled foods. Fortunately, there are some strategies you can use to make it easier to resist. For example, if you find yourself craving something sweet, find a gluten-free version. An even better choice would be to select a piece of fresh fruit, which has naturally occurring sugar. Sometimes the craving for something sweet indicates that you are in need of protein to help normalize your blood sugar. Try to find something that will provide the same satisfaction, but still maintain your gluten-free goals. When you do overcome temptation, reward yourself. Buy something nice, or do something special. This will help you reinforce the commitment you've made to improving your health and going gluten-free.

If the change feels overwhelming, you may be trying to do too much at once. Go back to basics. Simplify the aspects that cause you grief. Keep a positive outlook, and don't let friends or family members bring a negative attitude to your decision. As you dip into the 200 palate-pleasing recipes in Part 2, remember that this lifestyle change is all about you!

PART 2

Gluten-Free Recipes

BREAKFASTS

You don't have to give up your favorite breakfast foods when you give up gluten. You can even enjoy pancakes, waffles, and muffins as long as they're made with gluten-free, healthy flours. Add fresh fruit to any of these recipes to get your day off to a healthy start.

BREAKFASTS CONTENTS

BERRY OMELET

SERVES 4 | Calories: 563 | Protein: 16 grams | Carbohydrates: 26 grams | Fiber: 5 grams | Fat: 45 grams | Sodium: 227 milligrams

8 tablespoons unsalted butter or soy butter

2 cups raspberries

2 cups blueberries

2 cups strawberries (sliced ¼")

4 tablespoons raw brown sugar (optional)

12 eggs

4 tablespoons canola oil

1 orange (sliced ½" or cut into wedges)

1. Heat a medium sauté pan to medium high.

2. Add 4 tablespoons of butter, all the berries, and the sugar (if desired). Sauté berries for 1 minute, remove from the pan, then set aside.

3. Heat a 10" omelet pan to medium-high heat.

4. Meanwhile, crack the eggs and whip them in a small mixing bowl.

5. Add canola oil to the omelet pan and let heat for 30 seconds, then add the remaining butter. When the butter begins to melt, add ¼ of the whipped eggs.

6. Pull one side of the forming omelet toward the middle of the pan with a rubber spatula and let the uncooked eggs fill in the side. Continue until the entire bottom of the omelet has solidified. Add ¼ of the cooked berry mixture to one side of the omelet and fold over the opposite side to cover the berries.

7. Repeat 3 more times, garnish with orange wedges or slices, and serve.

GET THE EDGE

To make your egg dishes light and fluffy, bring the eggs to room temperature by placing them in a bowl and immersing them in cold water for about ten minutes before cooking.

SPINACH AND BAY SHRIMP OMELET

SERVES 4 | Calories: 704 | Protein: 62 grams | Carbohydrates: 4 grams | Fiber: 1 gram | Fat: 48 grams | Sodium: 850 milligrams

8 tablespoons soy butter

1 cup white button mushrooms (sliced thin)

3 garlic cloves (minced)

8 cups fresh spinach leaves (stems removed)

4 cups frozen or fresh bay shrimp (defrosted and rinsed)

Salt and pepper to taste

12 eggs

4 tablespoons canola oil

1 orange (sliced or cut into wedges)

1. Heat a small sauté pan to medium heat.

2. When the pan is hot, add half the butter and let melt.

3. Add the mushrooms and garlic. Sauté for 1 minute.

4. Add the spinach to the pan, and sauté for 2 minutes

5. Add the shrimp to the pan and sauté for 1 minute, then add salt and pepper and set aside.

6. Heat a 10" omelet pan to medium-high heat.

7. Meanwhile, crack the eggs and beat them in a small mixing bowl.

8. Add canola oil to the omelet pan and let heat for 30 seconds, then add the remaining butter. When the butter begins to melt, add ¼ of the eggs.

9. Pull one side of the forming omelet toward the middle of the pan with a rubber spatula and let the uncooked eggs fill in the side. Continue this process until the entire bottom of the omelet has solidified.

10. Add the spinach and shrimp mixture to one side of the omelet and fold over the opposite side to cover the mixture.

11. Repeat 3 more times, garnish with orange wedges or slices, and serve.

GET THE **EDGE**

Research indicates that people on a low-calorie diet who eat an egg along with their regular breakfast, three days per week, lose twice as many pounds as those who eat the same number of calories but don't include an egg with their morning meal. Why? One reason is that egg protein is filling, so you tend to eat less later on in the day.

BLUEBERRY PANCAKES

SERVES 4 | Calories: 426 | Protein: 19 grams | Carbohydrates: 48 grams | Fiber: 10 grams | Fat: 19 grams | Sodium: 1142 milligrams

4 cups garbanzo GF flour

1 teaspoon baking soda

4 tablespoons baking powder

4 tablespoons brown sugar

2 teaspoons salt

1 tablespoon cinnamon

8 eggs

2 tablespoons vanilla flavoring (not extract)

8 tablespoons canola oil

4 cups soy milk

2 cups blueberries

1 navel orange (sliced) for garnish

1. Heat a pancake griddle or skillet to 375°F.

2. Combine the flour, baking soda, baking powder, sugar, salt, and cinnamon in a mixing bowl.

3. In a separate bowl combine the eggs, vanilla flavoring, oil, and milk. Add to dry ingredients and mix just until dry ingredients are moistened. Carefully fold in blueberries.

4. Pour batter, ½ cup at a time, onto the hot griddle. Cook until bubbles appear across the surface of each pancake and the bottoms are browned, then flip over and cook one or two minutes or until pancakes are firm to the touch. Place on serving plate, garnish with navel orange slices, and serve.

GET THE **EDGE**

Garbanzo bean flour is made by grinding garbanzo beans (sometimes called chickpeas or cici) to a fine flour that is used by itself or blended with other bean flours. Garbanzo bean flour is an excellent substitute for the gluten-containing flours that are usually used for baking. This flour is a good source of protein and dietary fiber and, in addition to being gluten-free, it also contains no cholesterol, sodium, or saturated fat.

CREPES WITH PEACH SAUCE

SERVES 4 | Calories: 283 | Protein: 7 grams | Carbohydrates: 49 grams | Fiber: 4 grams | Fat: 7 grams | Sodium: 146 milligrams

2 tablespoons cornstarch

¼ cup cold water

2 peaches, blanched, peeled, and sliced

Juice of ½ lemon

1 teaspoon hot red pepper sauce, or to taste

½ cup sugar

Plenty of freshly ground black pepper

8 GF Crepes (see recipe in Sauces, Stocks, and Special Additions)

8 teaspoons mascarpone or cream cheese

1. Preheat oven to 300°F.

2. Mix the cornstarch in cold water until very smooth. Place in a saucepan with the peaches, lemon juice, hot sauce, and sugar. You may need to add some more water if the peaches are not very juicy. Bring to a boil, stirring constantly, until very thick and syrupy. Taste for seasonings and add black pepper to taste.

3. Lay the crepes on a baking sheet, spread with the cheese, and roll up. Use nonstick spray on a pie pan or baking dish.

4. Arrange the rolls, seam-side down, in the pan and bake for 10–15 minutes or until the crepe rolls are hot. Serve with the peach syrup.

GET THE **EDGE**

When you blanch a peach, a tomato, or a nectarine, you plunge it into boiling water for a minute. You don't cook it; you just loosen the skin. If you are blanching a great many pieces, have a colander next to your pot of boiling water and a pot of ice water in the sink. Use a slotted spoon to remove the fruit from the boiling water, put it into the colander, and then plunge the colander into the ice water. After the fruit is cool enough to handle, slip off the skin and cut it up.

SHIRRED EGGS WITH MUSHROOM AND SPINACH TOPPING

SERVES 4 | Calories: 252 | Protein: 15 grams | Carbohydrates: 2 grams | Fiber: <1 gram | Fat: 21 grams | Sodium: 368 milligrams

8 extra-large eggs

Salt and pepper to taste

4 tablespoons butter

4 cups fresh spinach, sautéed in butter

1 cup white button mushrooms (cleaned, small dice, sautéed in butter)

1. Preheat the oven to 350°F.

2. Prepare 8 small 4-ounce ramekins or 6 larger 6-ounce ones with nonstick spray. Place the ramekins on a cookie sheet. Break 1 egg into each of 8 small ramekins, or 2 eggs into each of 4 large.

3. Sprinkle the eggs with salt and pepper and dot with butter.

4. Top with spinach and mushrooms and bake for 8–12 minutes. Serve immediately.

SWEET POTATO FRITTATA WITH GOAT CHEESE AND HERBS

SERVES 4 | Calories: 386 | Protein: 22 grams | Carbohydrates: 11 grams | Fiber: 1 gram | Fat: 28 grams | Sodium: 701 milligrams

4 teaspoons butter

1 large sweet potato, peeled

Salt and pepper to taste

6 eggs

8 ounces goat cheese

6 sage leaves, minced

Fresh herbs and extra cheese to garnish

1. Using a mandoline, slice the potato as thinly as possible. Prepare a heavy 12" pan, first with nonstick spray, then with butter.

2. Add the potatoes, making a thin layer, and season with salt and pepper. Cook over medium heat for 10 minutes—this will be the crust.

3. Beat the eggs well; add the cheese and minced sage. Pour over the potatoes and turn down heat to the lowest possible setting. Cook for 10 minutes.

4. When the eggs have set, run the frittata under the broiler until golden brown on top. Cut into wedges and serve at once with garnishes.

SCRAMBLED EGGS WITH LEEKS

SERVES 4 | Calories: 266 | Protein: 19 grams | Carbohydrates: 7 grams | Fiber: <1 gram | Fat: 17 grams | Sodium: 531 milligrams

12 eggs

Canola oil spray

1 tablespoon soy butter

2 cups fresh leeks (cleaned, halved, sliced thin)

1 cup fresh cilantro (chopped medium)

Salt and pepper to taste

1 orange (cut into wedges)

1. Heat a large sauté pan to medium-high heat.

2. Crack the eggs into a medium mixing bowl and whip.

3. Spray the sauté pan with canola oil and then add the butter. When the butter begins to melt, add the leeks, then cook for 1 minute.

4. Pour in the eggs and stir in a circular motion with a rubber spatula to blend them with the leeks.

5. Add the cilantro, salt, and pepper.

6. Divide evenly onto 4 plates, garnish with orange wedges, and serve.

BREAKFAST PARFAIT

SERVES 4 | Calories: 614 | Protein: 16 grams | Carbohydrates: 80 grams | Fiber: 10 grams | Fat: 15 grams | Sodium: 125 milligrams

3½ ounces vanilla low-fat yogurt (or flavor of your choice)

3 cups Green Mountain Granola (see recipe below)

2 cups strawberries, 2 tablespoons per layer (sliced)

2 cups blueberries, 2 tablespoons per layer

2 cups raspberries, 2 tablespoons per layer

4 mint sprigs

1. In 4" parfait glass or a regular tall glass add 2 tablespoons of the yogurt, 2 tablespoons of the granola, and 2 tablespoons of the strawberries.

2. Add another layer of yogurt, another layer of granola, and the blueberries.

3. Add another layer of yogurt and then another layer of granola.

4. Top with the raspberries and mint sprig and serve.

GET THE **EDGE**

A breakfast parfait is a light and flavorful dish that provides many essential nutrients. The yogurt contains protein and calcium, and the fresh berries are loaded with fiber and antioxidants. To get the most out of this dish, check labels for gluten-containing ingredients and buy organic yogurt, which is hormone- and pesticide-free and has no antibiotics.

GREEN MOUNTAIN GRANOLA

SERVES 4 | Calories: 353 | Protein: 9 grams | Carbohydrates: 65 grams | Fiber: 7 grams | Fat: 8 grams | Sodium: 50 milligrams

Canola oil spray

3 cups GF rolled oats

½ cup chopped raw almonds

½ cup sunflower seeds

¼ cup oat bran

1 tablespoon ground cinnamon

1 cup raisins

1 cup red currants

¾ cup honey

½ cup apple cider

½ tablespoon vanilla extract

2 teaspoons canola oil

2 teaspoons grated orange zest

2 tablespoons fresh orange juice

1. Preheat oven to 250°F.

2. Lightly coat a baking sheet with oil spray.

3. In a large mixing bowl, combine rolled oats, almonds, sunflower seeds, bran, cinnamon, raisins, and red currants.

4. In medium-size mixing bowl, whisk together the honey, apple cider, vanilla, and oil until the honey is thoroughly incorporated. Add the orange zest and orange juice.

5. Add the wet ingredients to the dry ingredients and combine well.

6. Spread the granola evenly over the baking sheet and bake for 1½ to 2 hours, checking every 15 or so minutes. When the granola begins to turn golden brown, turn it over gently with a spatula. When golden and dry, scrape onto a cool baking sheet and set aside to cool. Granola will crisp as it cools. Store the granola in a reusable container for up to 2 months.

BREAKFAST RISOTTO

SERVES 4 | Calories: 475 | Protein: 13 grams | Carbohydrates: 61 grams | Fiber: 6 grams | Fat: 21 grams | Sodium: 415 milligrams

2 cups arborio rice

2 cups vanilla soy milk

1 cup raisins

½ cup gluten-free nonfat plain or vanilla yogurt

1 tablespoon cinnamon (ground)

2 tablespoons soy butter

½ teaspoon salt

1 cup slivered almonds

1. Heat a medium-size saucepan to medium-high heat. Add the rice and 1 cup of milk to the pot and cook until the rice absorbs the milk.

2. Add the remaining milk and stir until completely absorbed.

3. Add the raisins, yogurt, cinnamon, butter, salt, and almonds to the pot and stir to combine. Divide the risotto into 4 serving bowls and serve.

GET THE **EDGE**

Risotto is commonly used for an entrée mixed with vegetables, but this creamy type of rice can also be enjoyed for breakfast. So many people add refined sugar to their hot cereal, which actually makes a healthy meal unhealthy. You don't have to add extra sugar to this risotto, however. You can serve it like a hot cereal with fresh fruit to add natural sweetness.

BREAKFAST TORTILLAS

SERVES 4 | Calories: 336 | Protein: 15 grams | Carbohydrates: 25 grams | Fiber: 4 grams | Fat: 20 grams | Sodium: 318 milligrams

8 corn tortillas (lightly charred over gas burner, wrapped in a kitchen towel to keep warm)

2 tablespoons canola oil

2 tablespoons unsalted or soy butter

8 medium whole white button mushrooms (cut into ¼" slices)

1 yellow onion (chopped medium)

1 cup tomato (small dice)

Salt and cracked black pepper to taste

8 eggs (beaten)

2 cups fresh cilantro (rinsed, chopped medium)

1. Heat a large sauté pan to medium heat and add the oil to the pan. Let heat for 20 seconds. Add the butter, mushrooms, onion, tomato, salt, and pepper.

2. Sauté the vegetables for 2 minutes until softened and then pour in the eggs. Scramble the eggs together with the vegetables. Cook the eggs to desired consistency and turn off heat, but do not remove from the pan.

3. Fill each tortilla with a generous amount of the egg mixture and top with a tablespoon of cilantro. Place two tortillas on each plate and serve with a large bowl of fresh-cut fruit.

GET THE **EDGE**

When you're trying to lose weight, it is so important to eat breakfast. Studies have shown that when people don't eat anything for breakfast they end up consuming more calories throughout the day. This is a perfect breakfast to take with you when you need to eat breakfast on your way to work or to an appointment.

SPINACH BENEDICT

SERVES 4 | Calories: 414 | Protein: 7 grams | Carbohydrates: 16 grams | Fiber: 2 grams | Fat: 36 grams | Sodium: 429 milligrams

Canola oil spray

1 18-ounce package prepared polenta (plain or garlic, cut into 8½" disks)

2 tablespoons canola oil

4 cups fresh spinach (rinsed, stemmed, chopped medium)

4 egg yolks

1 tablespoon lemon juice

8 tablespoons soy butter (melted)

1 tablespoon cayenne pepper (optional)

Salt and cracked black pepper to taste

GET THE **EDGE**

Traditionally, eggs Benedict is served on an English muffin with eggs and Canadian bacon. That is a fatty dish that may cause weight gain. This is a lower-fat and healthier version of this popular dish. The polenta becomes a substitute for the English muffin and the spinach stands in for the bacon.

1. Preheat oven to 425°F.

2. Spray a foil-lined baking sheet lightly with oil and place the polenta disks on it. Bake for 5–6 minutes or until the disks are lightly browned, then set aside.

3. Heat a large sauté pan to medium-high heat. Add the oil and heat for 20 seconds, then add the spinach. Sauté the spinach for about 3 minutes or until completely cooked through and set aside.

4. Add 4 cups of water to a medium-size pot. Heat until the water is barely simmering.

5. In a medium-size metal mixing bowl, combine egg yolks and lemon juice. Whisk until the mixture is smooth.

6. Place the bowl with the eggs over the pot containing simmering water. Continue to whisk rapidly. Be careful not to let the eggs get too hot or they will scramble.

7. Slowly drizzle in the melted butter and continue to whisk until the sauce is thickened.

8. Remove from the heat, whisk in the cayenne pepper and salt and pepper, then cover and set aside in a warm spot until ready to use. If the sauce gets too thick, whisk in a few drops of warm water before serving.

9. Place 2 polenta disks on each of 4 serving plates. Top with the egg and a generous pile of spinach and spoon a generous amount of sauce over each disk. Sprinkle with cayenne and serve.

ORANGE CORNMEAL BREAKFAST PORRIDGE

SERVES 4 | Calories: 440 | Protein: 6 grams | Carbohydrates: 102 grams | Fiber: 2 grams | Fat: 2 grams | Sodium: 495 milligrams

2 cups vanilla soy milk

2 cups water

1 large navel orange (zest removed, then peeled)

1 teaspoon sea salt

¾ cup cornmeal

½ cup low-fat plain yogurt (preferably Nogurt)

1 cup honey

1 cup mandarin oranges (for garnish)

1. Heat a medium saucepan to medium-high heat. Add the milk, water, zest, salt, and cornmeal and bring to a boil.

2. Lower heat to a simmer and whisk until porridge thickens. Let cool, then fold in the yogurt and honey.

3. Spoon an even amount of the porridge into 4 bowls, top with orange sections, and serve.

GET THE **EDGE**

Try swapping out yogurt for Nogurt, a new yogurt product that does not contain any soy, wheat, dairy, or synthetic food additives. It provides vitamins B1 and B3 as well as DHA, an omega-3 fatty acid that is usually found in fish oil supplements. It is available at some health food markets.

PINEAPPLE OATMEAL PANCAKES

SERVES 4 | Calories: 334 | Protein: 11 grams | Carbohydrates: 58 grams | Fiber: 8 grams | Fat: 8 grams | Sodium: 1198 milligrams

2 cups GF oatmeal

½ cup coconut (shredded)

2 tablespoons garbanzo flour

2 tablespoons raw brown sugar

1 tablespoon baking powder

½ teaspoon baking soda

1 teaspoon salt

2½ cups fresh pineapple (chopped small)

¾ cup vanilla soy milk

3 eggs (beaten)

Canola spray

Soy butter, pure maple syrup to taste

1. Combine the oatmeal, coconut, flour, sugar, baking powder, baking soda, and salt in your food processor. Pulse the ingredients several times to combine well.

2. Add the pineapple, milk, and eggs and pulse until the mixture is smooth. Let the batter rest for 3 minutes before making the pancakes.

3. Heat a large sauté pan or griddle to medium heat. Spray the pan/griddle with oil to cover evenly.

4. Ladle ¼ cup of the batter onto the cooking surface and cook until the pancakes are no longer wet on the edges and turn a light golden brown.

5. Flip the pancakes and continue cooking until golden brown. Repeat this process until 8 pancakes are made, then place two pancakes on each of the 4 serving plates.

6. Top each stack with a pat of soy butter and pure maple syrup, and serve.

GET THE **EDGE**

Most gluten-free pancake recipes are made with rice flour, but we prefer using gluten-free oatmeal because it has a wonderful nutty flavor. When buying the ingredients for this recipe, don't forget to buy gluten-free baking powder and baking soda. These products are sometimes cross-contaminated with gluten, so read the labels carefully.

PINEAPPLE, APPLE, AND MANDARIN ORANGE YOGURT SMOOTHIE

SERVES 4 | Calories: 296 | Protein: 8 grams | Carbohydrates: 33 grams | Fiber: 3 grams | Fat: 2 grams | Sodium: 106 milligrams

15-ounce can mandarin oranges (drained, 1 tablespoon of juice reserved)

32-ounce tub plain or organic orange yogurt (or Nogurt)

2 medium Red Delicious apples (peeled, cored, and diced medium)

2 cups fresh-cut pineapple

1½ cups crushed ice

4 mint sprigs

1. Add the oranges, juice, and yogurt to your food processor, then pulse several times until combined.

2. While the processor is running, add the apples and pineapple and blend until combined well.

3. Add the ice while the processor is running and blend for 30 seconds. Pour the smoothie into tall glasses, garnish with mint, and serve.

RED CURRANT AND CORN WAFFLES

SERVES 4 | Calories: 421 | Protein: 9 grams | Carbohydrates: 67 grams | Fiber: 4 grams | Fat: 14 grams | Sodium: 322 milligrams

1 cup GF all-purpose flour

1 cup cornmeal

2 teaspoons baking powder

Sea salt to taste

Real maple syrup to taste

1. In a large mixing bowl, combine the flour, cornmeal, baking powder, and salt. Whisk to combine.

2. Add the eggs, oil, and milk and whisk until smooth.

3. Next, using a rubber spatula, gently fold in the currants and corn.

4. Ladle the recommended amount of waffle batter onto the waffle iron according to the manufacturer's instructions. Close iron top and cook until the waffle is golden on both sides and is easily removed from iron. Repeat this process 3 more times and serve with real maple syrup.

SMOKED SALMON PANCAKE EGG

SERVES 4 | Calories: 395 | Protein: 32 grams | Carbohydrates: <1 gram | Fiber: 0 grams | Fat: 25 grams | Sodium: 2531 milligrams

Canola oil spray

4 tablespoons unsalted butter

8 eggs (beaten in batches of 2 per person)

16 smoked salmon strips (1"–2" wide, 3"–4" long)

Salt and pepper to taste

½ cup fresh chives (chopped medium)

1. Spray a 10" sauté or omelet pan with oil and bring it to medium heat. Add a tablespoon of butter to the pan and, once melted, add 2 beaten eggs.

2. While the eggs are congealing, lay 4 salmon strips evenly across the top of the "pancake."

3. Sprinkle with salt and pepper and continue cooking just until the edges of the "pancake" are brown. Slide onto a serving plate, top with chives, and serve. Repeat this process 3 more times.

SPICED APPLE OATMEAL

SERVES 4 | Calories: 246 | Protein: 6 grams | Carbohydrates: 42 grams | Fiber: 5 grams | Fat: 4 grams | Sodium: 320 milligrams

1 cup fresh apple cider or juice

1 teaspoon sea salt

2 cups gluten-free oatmeal (such as Bob's Red Mill Gluten-Free Steel Cut Oatmeal)

1 apple (your choice, peeled, cored, cut into bite-size pieces)

1 tablespoon unsalted butter

1 tablespoon cinnamon (ground)

1 teaspoon nutmeg

1 cup low-fat vanilla yogurt

1. Heat a medium saucepan to medium-high heat. Add the cider or juice, butter, and salt and bring to a boil.

2. Add the oatmeal and lower the heat to a simmer. Cook for 10–20 minutes depending on your desired consistency.

3. Add the spiced apples to the pan and fold into the oatmeal to combine well.

4. Divide the oatmeal evenly into 4 serving bowls, top each bowl with a dollop of yogurt, sprinkle with cinnamon and nutmeg, and serve.

STRAWBERRY BREAKFAST CREPES

SERVES 4 | Calories: 511 | Protein: 26 grams | Carbohydrates: 72 grams | Fiber: 15 grams | Fat: 12 grams | Sodium: 467 milligrams

1 cup water

4 tablespoons raw sugar

4 cups fresh strawberries (rinsed, topped, and cut into ¼" slices; reserve 4 whole strawberries for garnish)

2 tablespoons soy butter

8 egg whites (beaten)

2 cups vanilla soy milk

1 teaspoon sea salt

2 cups garbanzo flour

Canola oil spray

1 cup vanilla yogurt

1. Heat a medium-size saucepan to medium-high heat and add the water and sugar. Bring to a boil, then lower the heat and cook until mixture begins to thicken.

2. Add the strawberries and butter, then cook for 1 minute or until the strawberries begin to soften. Remove from the heat.

3. In a medium mixing bowl add the egg whites, milk, and salt, then whisk to combine well. Slowly pour in the flour and whisk vigorously to combine with the wet ingredients.

4. Heat a 10" crepe pan or nonstick sauté pan to medium heat. Spray the pan lightly with oil and pour in ¼ cup of crepe batter. Move the batter around the pan to cover the bottom evenly. Cook for about 2 minutes or until light brown, then turn over and cook for 1 minute more or until light brown. Slide crepe onto a serving plate. Repeat until you've made 8 crepes.

5. Spoon an equal amount of strawberries onto each crepe, fold the crepe over itself, cover with a generous dollop of yogurt, garnish with a strawberry, and serve.

SWEET POTATO HASH BROWN EGG CUPS

SERVES 4 | Calories: 436 | Protein: 7 grams | Carbohydrates: 22 grams | Fiber: 2 grams | Fat: 36 grams | Sodium: 220 milligrams

4 cups sweet potatoes (shredded)

1 cup canola oil

Salt and pepper to taste

1 small yellow onion (cut into ¼" slices)

8 eggs

½ cup fresh parsley (chopped fine)

GET THE **EDGE**

Sweet potatoes contain antioxidants and lots of nutrients such as vitamins A, C, and B6. These amazing attributes along with their sumptuous flavor make them a perfect choice for a healthy, gluten-free breakfast. The nice thing about baking the eggs directly in the potato is that you don't need to add any additional fat, making this recipe even healthier.

1. Preheat oven to 400°F.

2. Heat a large sauté pan to medium-high heat.

3. In a medium mixing bowl combine sweet potatoes, ¾ cup oil, salt, and pepper.

4. Combine the potato mixture so the oil coats the potatoes well.

5. Place the potato mixture in the sauté pan and press down the mixture with a spatula to form a fairly solid cake.

6. Cook until both sides are slightly browned and then transfer to the bowl the mixture came from to cool.

7. To the same sauté pan add remaining ¼ cup oil and the onions. Sauté the onions for 3–4 minutes, or until lightly browned and soft, then set aside.

8. Using a nonstick muffin tin, place an equal amount of potatoes into 8 molds and press down against the sides of each mold to form a cup.

9. Bake for 8 minutes or until golden brown. Remove from the oven and set aside.

10. Crack an egg into each potato cup and return to the oven for 3–4 minutes or until the eggs have set.

11. Remove from the oven and top each egg cup with an even amount of onions. Unmold 2 cups onto each serving plate, sprinkle with parsley, salt, and pepper, and serve.

TOFU OMELET WITH SPINACH, MUSHROOMS, PARMESAN CHEESE, AND GARLIC

SERVES 4 | Calories: 546 | Protein: 30 grams | Carbohydrates: 8 grams | Fiber: 2 grams | Fat: 45 grams | Sodium: 796 milligrams

4 tablespoons canola oil

4 cups fresh spinach (cleaned, stemmed, chopped medium)

4 garlic cloves (minced fine)

Salt and pepper to taste

Canola oil spray

4 tablespoons unsalted butter

1 16-ounce package regular tofu

8 large white button mushrooms (rinsed, cut into ¼" slices)

2 cups Parmigiano-Reggiano cheese (shaved)

1. Heat a medium-size sauté pan to medium heat. Add 2 tablespoons of oil and the spinach to the pan. Sauté the spinach for 2 minutes, then add the garlic, salt, and pepper and continue to cook for 1 more minute.

2. Remove the spinach mixture from the pan and set aside.

3. Heat an omelet pan or 10" sauté pan to medium-high heat. Spray the pan with oil and add 1 tablespoon of butter. Add ¼ of the tofu to the pan; flatten it out to cover the bottom of the pan and cook until lightly browned.

4. On the left half of the omelet add ¼ of the spinach, then top with ¼ of the mushrooms and then with ½ cup of cheese.

5. Let cook for 20 seconds, then fold the right half of the omelet over the left half and slide onto a serving plate. Repeat until you've made 4 omelets, and serve.

GET THE **EDGE**

A healthy breakfast that includes a good source of protein is imperative for concentration and peak performance throughout your day. This tofu omelet is a perfect departure from eating eggs as your source of protein for breakfast. Studies indicate that adding soy to the diet helps to reduce heart disease and certain types of cancer. It can also help to increase body density to prevent osteoporosis.

AUNT JUNO'S STUFFED FRENCH TOAST

SERVES 4 | Calories: 715 | Protein: 20 grams | Carbohydrates: 65 grams | Fiber: 9 grams | Fat: 44 grams | Sodium: 1597 milligrams

1 8-ounce container Tofutti cream cheese

16 slices GF bread

4 tablespoons raw brown sugar

2 cups fresh raspberries (rinsed)

4 tablespoons canola oil

4 eggs (beaten in a medium mixing bowl for dipping)

Pure maple syrup to taste

1. Spread a generous layer of cream cheese on each slice of bread, then sprinkle with brown sugar.

2. Top 8 of the slices with raspberries, then top with the remaining bread slices and press together. Set aside on a large serving plate.

3. Heat a large sauté pan to medium heat and add the oil. Let heat for 20 seconds.

4. Dunk a "raspberry sandwich" in the egg, then place it in the pan.

5. Cook "sandwiches" until golden brown on each side, then remove to a large paper towel–covered serving plate to drain. Repeat this process until a total of 8 French toasts are made. Place 2 French toasts on each of 4 serving plates and serve with pure maple syrup.

HORS D'OEUVRES

It is possible to host a cocktail party, or dressy dinner party, without your guests realizing that the food they are eating is completely gluten-free? Now you can prepare a beautiful selection of hors d'oeuvres for your guests to enjoy and no one will even suspect that they're gluten-free. After years of entertaining, I have learned that people really enjoy having a variety of hors d'oeuvres that, together, make a complete meal. Here you will find vast array to choose from so you don't miss any vital food groups.

HORS D'OEUVRES CONTENTS

CRAB EGG ROLLS

SERVES 4 | Calories: 459 | Protein: 19 grams | Carbohydrates: 37 grams | Fiber: 3 grams | Fat: 25 grams | Sodium: 1962 milligrams

3 cups canola oil

2 cups green cabbage (shredded)

1 cup green onion (topped, chopped medium)

1 tablespoon fresh ginger (minced fine)

3 garlic cloves (minced fine)

Salt and pepper to taste

2 cups bean sprouts

3 6-ounce cans of crabmeat (lump or fancy)

1 cup fresh cilantro (chopped fine)

4 tablespoons tamari sauce

8 rice spring roll wrappers

2 cups hoisin sauce

1. Heat a small sauté pan to medium heat. Add 2 tablespoons of the oil to the pan and heat for 30 seconds. Add the cabbage, onion, ginger, ½ of the garlic, salt, and pepper to taste. Add the sprouts. Sauté mixture for 3 minutes or until cabbage begins to soften.

2. Remove mixture to small mixing bowl and add crab, cilantro, and tamari and blend together.

3. Soak spring roll wrappers in tepid water for 3 seconds and remove to a dry plate. Add ½ of the mixture to the bottom ⅜ of the wrapper. Fold the sides over the mixture, then fold the bottom over the mixture and continue to roll the wrapper until the mixture is covered. Repeat the same process with the other wrappers and remove to a serving plate.

4. Add the remaining oil to a medium-size deep saucepan and heat to 350°F. Check heat with a deep-fry/candy thermometer. Add 2 egg rolls and fry for 6 minutes. Remove to a plate with paper towels to drain excess oil. When drained, cut the rolls in half diagonally, and place on serving plate. Repeat this process until all 8 egg rolls are complete.

5. In a small saucepan mix the hoisin sauce and the remaining garlic and heat on low heat until warm. Pour into a dipping bowl on the serving plate, arrange the rolls on the plate, and serve.

STUFFED MUSHROOMS

SERVES 4 | Calories: 126 | Protein: 2 grams | Carbohydrates: 7 grams | Fiber: 2 grams |
Fat: 10 grams | Sodium: 439 milligrams

12 "stuffable" large white button
mushrooms

2 tablespoons olive oil

¼ cup red onion

½ cup black olives (fine chopped)

½ cup green olives (fine chopped)

½ cup roasted red pepper (fine chopped)

1 garlic clove (minced)

1 tablespoon white balsamic vinegar

1 tablespoon dried oregano

Salt and pepper to taste

1. Preheat oven to 375°F.

2. With a sharp paring knife, trace the inside circumference of each mushroom and remove the inside to create a mushroom cup that you can now stuff with filling. Set aside on a baking pan covered with tin foil.

3. Heat a medium sauté pan to medium-high heat. Add oil to sauté pan. Then, add onion and sauté for 1 minute.

4. Add olives, red pepper, garlic, vinegar, and oregano and sauté for 1 minute.

5. Add salt and pepper and then set aside to cool.

6. Spoon the cooled mixture into each mushroom cup. Place the baking pan in the heated oven and bake for 15 minutes. Remove to serving plate, and serve.

GET THE **EDGE**

Mushrooms are a great source of riboflavin and they are also low in calories and high in fiber and amino acids. Raw mushrooms by themselves do not have an abundance of flavor, but they act as a natural sponge and absorb different oils and seasonings.

HERBED POLENTA STICKS

SERVES 4 | Calories: 174 | Protein: 5 grams | Carbohydrates: 9 grams | Fiber: <1 gram | Fat: 13 grams | Sodium: 185 milligrams

3 tablespoons extra-virgin olive oil

1 teaspoon oregano/Italian herb mixture

½ of an 18-ounce package of premade polenta

½ cup shredded soy mozzarella cheese

½ cup Italian parsley (fine chopped)

Salt and pepper to taste

1. Heat a medium sauté pan to medium heat.

2. Pour olive oil into a shallow dish, and add salt, pepper, and oregano/herb mixture. Slice the polenta, with a sharp knife, into 1"-thick disks. Dip each disk into the olive oil to cover, then add to the sauté pan and cook until golden brown on each side.

3. Remove to a plate with paper towels to absorb excess oil. When cool enough to handle, slice disks into ½-inch sticks. Sprinkle sticks with cheese and microwave for 30–45 seconds, until cheese melts. Then sprinkle with parsley and serve.

GET THE EDGE

Polenta is made from cornmeal and water, so it is naturally gluten-free. These polenta "sticks" can also be served with a salad or a lettuce wrap to take the place of French fries. You can make this recipe without the cheese and sprinkle Italian herbs on the polenta sticks instead.

TUNA TATAKI CUPS

SERVES 4 | Calories: 205 | Protein: 20 grams | Carbohydrates: 6 grams | Fiber: <1 gram | Fat: 11 grams | Sodium: 667 milligrams

6 ounces sushi grade ahi tuna (cut into ¼" cubes)

6 ounces sushi grade toro tuna (cut into ¼" cubes)

2 green onions (fine chopped)

2 tablespoons Mirin rice wine

1 teaspoon rice wine vinegar

1 teaspoon lemon juice

2 tablespoons canola oil

1 cucumber

8 ounces radish sprouts

1 teaspoon sea salt

1. In a medium-sized mixing bowl, combine the ahi and toro tuna and green onion.

2. In a small mixing bowl, whisk together the Mirin, rice wine vinegar, lemon juice, salt, and oil. Pour marinade over tuna mixture and coat the fish well. Cover bowl with plastic wrap and set aside for 20 minutes.

3. Lay the cucumber horizontally on its side. Trim each end and discard. Cut 1"-wide sections. Turn each section so they stand vertically upright. With a teaspoon, gently remove the seeds. Make sure to leave enough of the inside of the cucumber section, about ¼", to hold the tuna mixture. With a sharp knife, remove the skin. Leave ½" of the inside of the cucumber section on the bottom to form a cup.

4. Place the cucumber cups evenly on the serving plate. Spoon the marinated tuna mixture into each cup to the brim, top generously with sprouts, and serve.

TURKEY BURGER SLIDERS

SERVES 4 | Calories: 741 | Protein: 56 grams | Carbohydrates: 31 grams | Fiber: 4 grams | Fat: 42 grams | Sodium: 593 milligrams

32 ounces ground turkey

1 cup red onion (chopped fine)

1 cup fresh cilantro (chopped fine)

3 garlic clove (minced)

Salt and pepper to taste

8 slices rice bread

4 tablespoons canola oil

2 cups romaine lettuce (chopped fine)

1. Combine the turkey, onion, cilantro, and garlic in a medium-size mixing bowl, then add salt and pepper.

2. Mix the ingredients together with your hands and then create 8 mini burgers and set aside.

3. Lightly toast the rice bread, then cut out 2 circles from each slice of bread using a 3"-diameter cup or ring and set on serving plate.

4. Heat a medium-size sauté pan to medium-high heat.

5. Add the oil and, after 1 minute, sauté the burgers to desired doneness, or at least 2 minutes on each side.

6. Place a cooked mini burger on a bread circle, cover with lettuce, and cover with another bread circle. Repeat this process with all the mini burgers and serve.

GET THE EDGE

Ground turkey is an excellent way to make a burger without using red meat. To eliminate the higher fat content found in dark-meat turkey, ask your butcher or grocer to grind only white-meat turkey for you.

PARSNIP-STUFFED TOMATOES

SERVES 4 | Calories: 132 | Protein: 2 grams | Carbohydrates: 17 grams | Fiber: 3 grams | Fat: 6 grams | Sodium: 315 milligrams

2 large fresh parsnips (cut into 3" lengths, peeled and washed)

2 tablespoons unsalted butter or soy butter

1 small shallot (minced fine)

Salt and pepper to taste

½ cup plain soy milk

12 cherry tomatoes* (halved)

Note: Slightly larger vine tomatoes can be substituted for cherry tomatoes.

1. In a medium to large microwave-safe bowl, combine parsnips and butter.

2. Microwave on high for 4 minutes or until tender and set aside.

3. Combine parsnips, shallot, salt, and pepper in your food processor, then pulse the processor to break the parsnips into smaller pieces.

4. Through the top feeder of the processor, stream in the soy milk to desired consistency.

5. With processor still running, blend until fully puréed.

6. Taste the mixture, adjust flavors, and set aside to cool for 2 minutes. When cooled, transfer the parsnip mixture to a small zip-top bag and seal shut.

7. Take the butt end of a wooden cooking utensil and gently push in the inside of each cherry tomato to form a cavity to fill with the parsnip mixture.

8. On a serving plate, arrange all the cherry tomatoes. Snip one bottom corner of the zip-top bag, fill each tomato to the top with the parsnip mixture, and serve.

SPINACH AND MUSHROOM MEZZALUNAS

SERVES 4 | Calories: 441 | Protein: 21 grams | Carbohydrates: 48 grams | Fiber: 13 grams | Fat: 20 grams | Sodium: 211 milligrams

1 tablespoon unsalted butter or soy butter

4 cups fresh spinach (stems removed, chopped small)

2 cups garbanzo/fava flour

½ teaspoon salt

3 eggs

3 tablespoons olive oil plus a small amount for sprinkling

2 cups fresh white button mushrooms (chopped small)

1 clove garlic (minced fine)

1 shallot (minced fine)

Salt and pepper to taste

GET THE **EDGE**

This is a Roman homemade specialty that is normally packed with gluten from the semolina pasta flour that is traditionally used. The garbanzo/fava flour is an ideal substitute because it has a pleasant flavor and more nutritional value than other gluten-free flours. When preparing the spinach for cooking, be sure to completely remove the stems to optimize the flavor of the spinach.

1. Heat a medium sauté pan to medium-high heat. Add 1 cup of water and bring to a boil.

2. Add the butter and spinach leaves to the heated pan. Cook until spinach has been completely sautéed and all the water has evaporated, then remove to a small bowl and let cool.

3. In a food processor, add the flour and ½ teaspoon salt and pulse 5 times to blend. Add eggs to running processor and blend until a pasta ball forms. Remove the pasta to a small bowl, sprinkle olive oil on top, and cover with plastic wrap. Let pasta dough rest for 30 minutes in the refrigerator.

4. While pasta is resting, heat a medium sauté pan to medium-high heat. Add 2 tablespoons of olive oil and let heat for 1 minute. Add mushrooms and sauté for 2 minutes. Add the garlic, shallot, salt, pepper and well-drained spinach to the pan and sauté for 2 minutes.

5. Remove mixture to a small mixing bowl and let cool for 5 minutes. Save this pan for sautéing the mezzalunas.

6. Place pasta ball on GF floured surface and roll out until ⅛" thick with rolling pin or a pasta machine. Take a drinking glass 2–3" wide at the top and make circles of pasta from the sheet you rolled out. Place a teaspoon of filling on each circle, fold in half, and pinch the edges together to make a semicircle or mezzaluna.

7. Drop the mezzalunas in boiling water for 2 minutes and then drain completely. Gently sauté the mezzalunas in 1 tablespoon of oil, drain on paper towels, place on serving plate, and serve.

CORNMEAL ZUCCHINI DISKS

SERVES 4 | Calories: 281 | Protein: 14 grams | Carbohydrates: 35 grams | Fiber: 2 grams | Fat: 8 grams | Sodium: 540 milligrams

2 zucchinis (light green if possible)

2 cups cornmeal

2 tablespoons oregano (dried)

Salt and pepper to taste

Canola oil spray

1 egg (beaten with 1 teaspoon of water)

1 cup Parmigiano-Reggiano cheese (grated fine)

1. Preheat oven to 400°F.

2. With a sharp knife, cut each zucchini into ½" disks, on the bias diagonally.

3. In a small mixing bowl combine the cornmeal, oregano, salt, and pepper and set aside.

4. Line a baking sheet with foil, then spray with oil.

5. Roll the zucchini in the cornmeal mixture, then the egg, then the cornmeal again and place on the baking sheet. Repeat this process with all the zucchini disks.

6. Sprinkle a generous amount of cheese over each disk and place the baking sheet in the oven for 10–12 minutes. Remove from the oven, place the zucchini on a serving dish, and serve.

MINI CORN TORTILLAS WITH CILANTRO CHICKEN

SERVES 4 | Calories: 201 | Protein: 15 grams | Carbohydrates: 1 gram | Fiber: 1 gram | Fat: 7 grams | Sodium: 376 milligrams

4 GF corn tortillas

2 tablespoons canola oil

1 cup fresh cilantro (chopped fine) plus ½ cup for garnish

1 cup soy cream

1 tablespoon lime juice

2 tablespoons lime zest

Salt and pepper to taste

1 8-ounce chicken breast (boneless, skinless, cooked, cut into small dice)

1. Heat a large sauté pan to medium heat.

2. With a sturdy drinking glass or 2" ring cutter, cut each tortilla into 3 disks.

3. Add the oil to the pan and heat for 20 seconds. Lay the disks in the pan and cook both sides for 30 seconds and remove to a large paper towel–covered plate to drain.

4. In a small mixing bowl combine the cilantro, cream, juice, lime zest, salt, and pepper. Stir well to combine with wooden spoon. Add the chicken and stir to combine.

5. After the mini tortillas are drained, arrange them evenly on the plate and top each one with chicken mixture. Garnish each tortilla with cilantro and serve.

GET THE **EDGE**

It's important to note that you won't find anything made with beef in this book. Beef has high amounts of saturated fat, which can lead to weight gain or make it more difficult to lose weight.

SWEET POTATO CAKES WITH CRAB AIOLI

SERVES 4 | Calories: 506 | Protein: 14 grams | Carbohydrates: 4 grams | Fiber: <1 gram | Fat: 48 grams | Sodium: 1035 milligrams

2 cups sweet potato (peeled, shredded, drained well with paper towels)

Salt and pepper to taste

3 tablespoons canola oil

1 cup lump crabmeat

Basic Aioli (see recipe in Sauces, Stocks, and Special Additions)

½ cup chives (chopped small)

1. Heat a large sauté pan to medium heat.

2. Combine the potatoes, salt and pepper, and 2 tablespoons of oil in a small mixing bowl. Stir well with tablespoon.

3. Fill the spoon with a generous amount of potato and add to the pan. Sauté the cakes until they are browned on both sides, or about 3 minutes. Remove to a paper towel to drain and set aside. Repeat until all eight cakes are browned and crispy.

4. Gently fold the crab into the aioli and combine for 10 seconds.

5. Place potato cakes on a serving plate. Top each cake with a dollop of the crab mixture, sprinkle with chives, and serve.

TURKEY MINI "CORN DOGS"

SERVES 4 | Calories: 342 | Protein: 25 grams | Carbohydrates: 16 grams | Fiber: 3 grams | Fat: 19 grams | Sodium: 678 milligrams

1 lb. ground turkey (shape into 2" long x 1" wide hot-dog shape)

2 tablespoons canola oil

Celery salt to taste

Black pepper to taste

1 18-ounce package prepared polenta (plain or garlic flavor)

½ cup GF mustard (yellow or brown)

Canola oil spray

1. Preheat oven to 425°F.

2. Heat a medium-size sauté pan to medium heat. Add the oil. Season the turkey "dogs" with celery salt and pepper and place into pan.

3. Sauté the "dogs" until browned on both sides and remove to a paper towel–covered plate to drain and cool.

4. Line a baking sheet with foil and spray lightly with oil. Mold a generous amount of polenta around each cooled "dog" and place on the baking sheet. Cook in oven for 10–12 minutes or until the polenta is lightly browned.

5. Remove the baking sheet from the oven, place the "corn dogs" on a large serving plate, spread some mustard on each, and serve.

ZUCCHINI STICKS

SERVES 4 | Calories: 274 | Protein: 12 grams | Carbohydrates: 10 grams | Fiber: 3 grams | Fat: 22 grams | Sodium: 407 milligrams

3 large zucchinis

3 garlic cloves (minced fine)

1 tablespoon oregano (dried)

4 tablespoons canola oil

Salt and pepper to taste

1 cup GF Parmesan cheese (grated fine)

1. Preheat oven to 375°F.

2. To prepare your zucchini, first trim off the ends, then cut them each in half lengthwise. Then quarter them by cutting the halves in half. Then cut the quarters in half widthwise so you wind up with 8 separate "sticks" of zucchini.

3. In a medium mixing bowl combine the zucchini, garlic, oregano, oil, and salt and pepper to taste and, with your hands, toss the zucchini well to coat.

4. On a foil-lined baking sheet, lay out the tossed zucchini evenly. Spoon grated cheese generously over each "stick," reserving a small amount of cheese for garnish, and bake for 15 minutes.

5. Sprinkle with a pinch or two of cheese and serve.

BAKED GOAT CHEESE, FIG, AND HONEY TARTLETS

SERVES 4 | Calories: 675 | Protein: 22 grams | Carbohydrates: 86 grams | Fiber: 9 grams | Fat: 28 grams | Sodium: 699 milligrams

1 tablespoon yeast

1½ cups water

1 cup garbanzo/fava flour

2 eggs (beaten well)

3 tablespoons canola oil

Salt and pepper to taste

1 cup cornmeal

Canola oil spray

1 8-ounce goat cheese log (plain, not herbed, room temperature)

1 tablespoon fresh thyme

4 fresh figs (stemmed, chopped small)

½ cup honey

GET THE EDGE

This recipe will be appreciated by even the most discerning gourmand. The marriage of the cheese, figs, and honey is esoteric and very interesting to the palate. Pair these tartlets with a great port wine.

1. Preheat oven to 425°F.

2. In a medium-size mixing bowl add the yeast and water, heated to 105–110°F. Gently blend together well and let rest for 20 seconds.

3. Proceed to add the oil and eggs to the bowl and stir well to combine. Stir in 1 cup cornmeal, then add salt and pepper and cornmeal. Wet your hands and mix to create the dough ball.

4. Cover the bowl with plastic wrap and let the dough rise for 20 minutes or until doubled in size.

5. Spray a baking sheet with a light layer of oil. When the dough has finished rising, add it to the baking sheet. With continually wet hands, spread the dough out across the baking sheet until you achieve a perfectly even thickness. Bake for 8–9 minutes or until the dough is cooked through.

6. Remove from the oven, let cool for 5 minutes and, with a pizza cutter or sharp knife, cut the pizza into 16 equal squares.

7. In a medium-size mixing bowl, add the goat cheese and thyme. With a fork, combine the cheese and the thyme well. Add the chopped figs and combine until blended well.

8. Place an equal amount of the cheese mixture on each square and drip a teaspoon of honey over the cheese.

9. Bake for 5 minutes, then let the squares cool for 2 minutes. Remove to a large serving plate and serve.

CRAB AND GUACAMOLE MINI TORTILLAS

SERVES 4 | Calories: 367 | Protein: 25 grams | Carbohydrates: 22 grams | Fiber: 8 grams | Fat: 20 grams | Sodium: 1515 milligrams

2 ripe avocados (meat removed to a small mixing bowl)

1 garlic clove (minced fine)

1 tablespoon lime juice

1 cup fresh cilantro (chopped small) plus ½ cup for garnish

Salt and pepper to taste

2 cups crabmeat

1 tablespoon olive oil

1 Roma tomato (cut into small dice)

4 corn tortillas

1. Turn the flame on your gas grill or stove to medium high or preheat your oven to 425°F.

2. To make the guacamole, mash the avocado meat with a fork until it completely breaks down. Add the garlic, lime juice, cilantro, salt, and pepper to the mixing bowl, combine the ingredients well, and set aside.

3. In another small mixing bowl, add the crab, oil, tomato, salt, and pepper, then combine well.

4. Using a 3" ring cutter, cut 3 circles out of each corn tortilla and place on a plate. Using cooking tongs, carefully place each "mini tortilla" over the flame of your gas grill or stove and lightly char both sides. If you're using your oven, place tortillas on a baking sheet and bake for 3 minutes.

5. Lay out the charred "mini tortillas" on a large serving plate. Place a tablespoon of the crab mixture on each tortilla and then top the crab with a dollop of guacamole.

6. Sprinkle cilantro on top of the guacamole and serve.

GET THE **EDGE**

Do you ever wonder how many hors d'oeuvres to serve at a party? The number of hors d'oeuvres you need depends on the time frame of the cocktail hour and whether a meal will be served following the cocktail hour. If you are not serving dinner, plan for ten to twelve pieces per person. If you are planning a full dinner following the cocktail hour, plan for three to four pieces per person.

PARMESAN CRISPS CAPRISI

SERVES 4 | Calories: 583 | Protein: 28 grams | Carbohydrates: 4 grams | Fiber: <1 gram | Fat: 51 grams | Sodium: 1036 milligrams

Canola oil spray

2 cups Parmigiano-Reggiano cheese (shaved or grated)

2 Roma tomatoes (cut into ¼" slices)

8 slices fresh mozzarella cheese (milk, tapioca, or soy)

1 cup fresh basil leaves (stemmed, shredded)

Salt and pepper to taste

½ cup extra-virgin olive oil

1. Preheat oven to 425°F.
2. Line a baking sheet with foil and spray lightly with oil.
3. Place 16 piles of Parmigiano-Reggiano cheese evenly on the baking sheet and bake for 10–12 minutes or until melted into disks.
4. Remove from oven and cool for 5 minutes.
5. Place disks on a large serving plate and spread them out evenly. Top each disk with tomato, then mozzarella cheese, then basil, a little salt and black pepper, and finally a drizzle of olive oil. Serve.

GET THE **EDGE**

Parmesan cheese is made from milk and does not contain wheat, barley, or rye. Some grated cheeses are coated with modified food starch to keep the pieces from sticking together, but I have never found this problem with Parmesan cheese.

STUFFED ROASTED BABY BELL PEPPERS

SERVES 4 | Calories: 189 | Protein: 14 grams | Carbohydrates: 13 grams | Fiber: 3 grams | Fat: 9 grams | Sodium: 292 milligrams

Canola oil spray

12–16 baby bell peppers

16-ounce log of fresh ricotta cheese (low-fat)

½ cup fresh basil leaves (stemmed, chopped fine) plus 3–4 leaves for garnish

Salt and pepper to taste

1. Preheat oven to 450°F.

2. Line a baking sheet with foil and spray lightly with oil. Place the peppers on the baking sheet, evenly spaced, and bake for 10 minutes or until completely cooked through. Set aside to cool for 7–10 minutes.

3. In a food processor, add the cheese, basil, salt, and pepper. Pulse the processor about 20 times or until the ingredients are blended well.

4. When the peppers are cool, remove the tops with a sharp knife and discard. Clean out the insides with a small spoon and discard.

5. Fill each of the peppers with the cheese mixture and place on a large serving plate. Garnish with basil leaves and serve.

BALSAMIC GLAZED SALMON SKEWERS

SERVES 4 | Calories: 393 | Protein: 30 grams | Carbohydrates: 44 grams | Fiber: 1 gram | Fat: 9 grams | Sodium: 86 milligrams

1 cup balsamic vinegar

Salt and pepper to taste

1 tablespoon water

½ cup raw sugar

2 8-ounce fresh salmon fillets (cut length-wise into ¼'" strips)

1 zucchini (cut into 16½"-wide coins)

1 red onion (cut into 1"-wide quarters)

16 wooden skewers (8" long, like satay sticks, soaked in water for 20 minutes)

Canola oil spray

1. Preheat oven to 375°F.

2. Heat a small saucepan to medium heat. Add the balsamic vinegar, salt, pepper, water, and sugar to the pan and stir to combine. Cook the mixture until it begins to thicken, or about 3–4 minutes, then remove it from the heat.

3. On a large plate, lay out the salmon strips. Proceed to slide a zucchini coin and then an onion quarter onto each skewer. Then follow with a salmon strip skewered in three places. Finish the skewer with another onion quarter and another zucchini coin. Continue this process with each skewer and lay them out evenly on a lightly sprayed, foil-lined baking sheet.

4. With a cooking brush, generously paint the balsamic sauce on both sides of the salmon and vegetables. Bake for 8–10 minutes or until the skewers are bubbling hot. Remove from the oven, place the skewers on a large serving plate, and serve.

GET THE EDGE

If you're grilling the salmon, be sure to know where the hot spots are located on your grill and place all the salmon on the hot spots when cooking. Salmon burns easily, so don't walk away from the grill when cooking.

GRILLED PINEAPPLE LOGS WITH SHRIMP AND ROASTED RED PEPPERS

SERVES 4 | Calories: 361 | Protein: 3 grams | Carbohydrates: 11 grams | Fiber: 1 gram | Fat: 35 grams | Sodium: 32 milligrams

½ cup canola oil

1 fresh pineapple (trimmed and cut into 8 "logs," each 3" x 1")

8 large shrimp (peeled, deveined, tails off)

4 tablespoons unsalted butter (melted)

3 tablespoons paprika

Salt and pepper to taste

1 jar roasted red peppers (cut into ½"-wide strips)

8 toothpicks (2" long)

1. Heat your outdoor or indoor grill to medium heat and brush with canola oil.

2. Coat the pineapple logs and the shrimp with the melted butter using a cooking brush, then sprinkle with paprika, salt, and pepper.

3. Gently grill the pineapple and shrimp for 2 minutes per side, then place on a large serving plate.

4. Place a pepper strip on top of each pineapple log and then top with a shrimp. Attach shrimp and pepper strip to pineapple with a toothpick. Repeat this process until all are assembled, and serve.

SMOKEY ASIAN CORN FRITTERS

SERVES 4 | Calories: 255 | Protein: 5 grams | Carbohydrates: 27 grams | Fiber: 2 grams | Fat: 15 grams | Sodium: 528 milligrams

½ cup cornmeal

Salt

White, black, or cayenne pepper to taste (cayenne is hottest!)

1 tablespoon cumin (ground, toasted in a small pan for 30–45 seconds)

2 egg whites

1 tablespoon tamari

1 ear of fresh corn (kernels trimmed from cob)

1 cup fresh cilantro (chopped fine), plus a few leaves for garnish

2 green onions (top removed, cut on the bias into ½" slices)

2 garlic cloves (minced fine)

4 tablespoons canola oil

1. In a medium-size mixing bowl combine the cornmeal, salt, pepper, and cumin.

2. Add the egg whites, garlic, and tamari to the bowl and blend well.

3. Fold the corn, cilantro, and onions into the cornmeal mixture.

4. Heat a large sauté pan to medium-high heat and add the oil. Heat for 30–45 seconds, then add 2–3" dollops of the fritter batter to the pan with a large metal spoon, making sure the fritters are not too close to each other. Sauté until golden brown on both sides and remove to a paper towel–covered plate to drain.

5. Continue until all the batter is used. Let cool for 3 minutes and serve.

GRILLED CHICKEN AND ARTICHOKE MINI SKEWERS

SERVES 4 | Calories: 441 | Protein: 32 grams | Carbohydrates: 4 grams | Fiber: 2 grams |
Fat: 33 grams | Sodium: 574 milligrams

16 long toothpicks (4" long, soaked in water for 20 minutes)

1 15-ounce can or jar of artichoke hearts (cut in half)

2 8-ounce chicken breasts (boneless, skinless, cut into ½" strips)

3 tablespoons paprika

3 tablespoons oregano (dried)

Salt and cracked black pepper to taste

½ cup olive oil

½ cup Parmesan cheese for garnish (optional)

1. Heat your indoor or outdoor grill to medium heat. On a large plate, assemble the skewers by sliding a piece of artichoke onto the middle of the toothpick and then spearing one end of the chicken on each end so the chicken surrounds the artichoke.

2. Sprinkle with paprika, oregano, and salt and pepper to taste on both sides.

3. With a cooking brush, coat each skewer on both sides with oil. Place the skewers on the grill for 2–3 minutes per side or until completely cooked through. Remove to a serving plate, sprinkle with cheese, and serve.

SICILIAN EGGPLANT ROLLS

MAKES 10 TO 15 ROLLS | Calories: 533 | Protein: 16 grams | Carbohydrates: 29 grams | Fiber: 8 grams | Fat: 41 grams | Sodium: 805 milligrams

1 medium eggplant (about 1 pound), peeled

Salt

½ cup olive oil

½ cup garbanzo flour

1 cup ricotta cheese

¼ cup Sicilian olives, pitted and chopped

¼ cup Parmesan cheese

GET THE **EDGE**

Eggplant can be sliced thinly lengthwise or crosswise and then broiled or baked. Salting and stacking eggplant slices under a weight will drain off the bitterness that some seem to harbor. Be sure to use a plate with steep sides or a soup bowl under the eggplant—some give off a lot of juice when salted.

1. Cut the eggplant in very thin (⅛") slices with a mandoline. Sprinkle a pinch of salt on both sides of each slice and stack them on a plate; let sit under a weight for ½ hour to let the brown juices out.

2. Preheat oven to 300°F.

3. Pat the eggplant slices dry with paper towels.

4. Heat the oil to 300°F. Dip the slices in flour and fry until almost crisp, about 2 minutes per side.

5. Drain the slices and then place a spoonful of the ricotta cheese and some chopped olive on the end of each slice. Roll and secure with a toothpick.

6. Sprinkle the rolls with Parmesan cheese and bake for 9 minutes. Serve warm.

SPICY GORGONZOLA DIP WITH RED PEPPER "SPOONS"

YIELDS 2 CUPS | Calories: 200 | Protein: 5 grams | Carbohydrates: 6 grams | Fiber: 1 gram | Fat: 17 grams | Sodium: 598 milligrams

6 ounces Gorgonzola cheese, at room temperature

½ cup Homemade GF Mayonnaise (see recipe in Sauces, Stocks, and Special Additions)

4 ounces Tofutti cream cheese, at room temperature

2 ounces roasted red peppers (jarred is fine)

2 teaspoons fresh chopped herbs (such as oregano, basil, and chives)

Salt, black pepper, and Tabasco sauce to taste

4 sweet red bell peppers

1. Put all but the red peppers into the food processor and blend until smooth. Scrape into a serving bowl.

2. Wash, core, and seed the red bell peppers, and then cut into chunks (these will be your "spoons"). Place the red pepper spoons around the dip.

STUFFED ARTICHOKES WITH LEMON AND OLIVES

SERVES 8 | Calories: 224 | Protein: 6 grams | Carbohydrates: 26 grams | Fiber: 11 grams | Fat: 12 grams | Sodium: 521 milligrams

½ lemon

4 quarts water

4 large artichokes, trimmed and split lengthwise

1 cup cooked rice

10 green olives, chopped

10 kalamata olives, chopped

2 tablespoons minced parsley

3 tablespoons butter or margarine, melted

1 teaspoon garlic salt

Pepper to taste

1 egg, optional

1. Preheat the oven to 350°F.

2. Squeeze the lemon juice into 4 quarts water and then add the lemon half to the water, skin and all. Add the artichokes and boil for 20 minutes. Drain artichokes and lay out on a baking sheet, cut-side up.

3. Mix the rest of the ingredients (including the egg, if using) together in a large bowl.

4. Spoon the filling over the artichokes, pressing between the leaves. Bake for 15 minutes, until hot.

GET THE **EDGE**

When buying artichokes, look for ones that are tightly closed. Use a pair of kitchen scissors to clip the sharp points off the leaves. You can use a knife to cut off the tops. Artichokes can be stuffed with many kinds of delicious foods to make a hearty dish. If you eat fish, try salmon mixed with rice for an excellent stuffing.

SOUPS AND SALADS

It can be very difficult to find gluten-free soups that taste good and are not loaded with sodium, but all the soup recipes here use only fresh whole foods and natural spices. You will also find a wide variety of salads that are refreshing and packed with flavor. The soups and salads in this section can be eaten on their own for lunch or try any of these great gluten-free soups and salads to complement any of the dishes in the Entrées section of the book.

SOUPS AND SALADS CONTENTS

RED AND YELLOW ROASTED PEPPER SOUP

SERVES 4 | Calories: 169 | Protein: 3 grams | Carbohydrates: 25 grams | Fiber: 8 grams | Fat: 8 grams | Sodium: 206 milligrams

4 cups GF Homemade Chicken Stock or GF Homemade Vegetable Stock (see recipes in Sauces, Stocks, and Special Additions)

2 red bell peppers (roasted and skin, insides removed)

2 yellow bell peppers (roasted and skin, insides removed)

1 ripe avocado (mashed)

1 cup fresh cilantro (rough chopped)

2 tablespoons lime juice

Salt and pepper to taste

1. Heat 2 separate small saucepans, to medium-high heat. Add 16 ounces of stock to each. Bring to a simmer.

2. Add red pepper to one saucepan and yellow pepper to the other. With a hand blender, blend both the red and yellow peppers in their separate pans. Turn heat to low.

3. In a small mixing bowl, stir avocado, cilantro, lime juice, salt, and pepper until combined.

4. To serve, simultaneously add a ladleful of each color soup to each side of a large soup bowl. The soup bowl should have half-and-half red and yellow pepper soup. Place a generous dollop of the avocado mixture in the center of the already poured soup, and garnish with a cilantro sprig. Repeat 3 times and serve.

GET THE **EDGE**

Most soup manufacturers add gluten-filled wheat flour to their products or fill them with pasta or barley. There are a few companies that make gluten-free soups, such as Progresso and Campbell's, but there is nothing better than homemade. This roasted pepper soup is full of thiamin, niacin, and folate and only takes about 20 minutes to prepare.

TOMATO BASIL SOUP

SERVES 4 | Calories: 112 | Protein: 2 grams | Carbohydrates: 21 grams | Fiber: 4 grams | Fat: 2 grams | Sodium: 511 milligrams

4 cups GF Homemade Vegetable Stock (see recipe in Sauces, Stocks, and Special Additions)

2 tablespoons fresh basil (stemmed, fine chopped; reserve a pinch for garnish)

1 teaspoon olive oil

16 ounces whole skinless tomatoes (fresh* or canned)

Salt and pepper to taste

Fresh Gluten-Free Croutons (see recipe in Sauces, Stocks, and Special Additions)

*Note: Remove the skin of fresh tomatoes by immersing them into boiling water for 2 minutes. Then immerse them in ice cold water and peel off the skin with your fingers.

1. Heat a medium-size saucepan to medium-high heat. Add stock, basil, oil, and tomatoes to the pan. Bring to a boil and then reduce to a simmer.

2. Using a hand or immersion blender, blend the mixture until it's smooth. Add salt and pepper.

3. Top with croutons, sprinkle with basil, and serve.

WHITE BEAN AND THYME SOUP

SERVES 4 | Calories: 277 | Protein: 12 grams | Carbohydrates: 47 grams | Fiber: 13 grams | Fat: 5 grams | Sodium: 885 milligrams

2 teaspoons olive oil

2 tablespoons fresh or dry thyme

2 garlic cloves (minced)

4 cups GF Homemade Chicken Stock (see recipe in Sauces, Stocks, and Special Additions)

2 15-ounce cans of white beans

Salt and pepper to taste

Fresh Gluten-Free Croutons (see recipe in Sauces, Stocks, and Special Additions)

1. Heat a medium saucepan to medium-high heat. Add oil, thyme, and garlic to the pan and stir.

2. After 30 seconds, add the stock and beans. Season with salt and pepper. Bring to a boil, then reduce to a simmer.

3. Let the soup cook for 15 minutes on low, then ladle into a bowl, top with croutons, sprinkle a pinch of thyme on top, and serve.

OYSTER STEW À LA GRAND CENTRAL OYSTER BAR

SERVES 4 | Calories: 259 | Protein: 11 grams | Carbohydrates: 25 grams | Fiber: <1 gram | Fat: 13 grams | Sodium: 557 milligrams

2 tablespoons unsalted butter

2 tablespoons Worcestershire sauce

1 cup bottled or fresh clam broth

2 tablespoons cornstarch mixed with 3 tablespoons cold water

1/8 teaspoon cayenne pepper

1 quart shucked oysters, drained

2 cups soy milk

1 cup soy cream

Sprinkle of celery salt and paprika

4 pats butter

Oyster crackers

1. Mix 2 tablespoons butter, Worcestershire, and clam broth together in a saucepan over medium heat for 1 minute. Whisk in the cornstarch/water mixture. Add the cayenne, oysters, milk, and cream.

2. Heat carefully over a low flame until quite thick, stirring frequently for about 10 minutes. Just before serving, sprinkle with celery salt and paprika, then float a pat of butter on top of each bowl. Serve with oyster crackers on the side.

YELLOW SQUASH AND APPLE SOUP

SERVES 4 | Calories: 310 | Protein: 2 grams | Carbohydrates: 45 grams | Fiber: 2 grams | Fat: 15 grams | Sodium: 126 milligrams

2 shallots, minced

1 Granny Smith apple, peeled, cored, and chopped

2 medium yellow squash, washed and chopped

4 tablespoons butter

3 cups fresh orange juice

1 cup apple juice

Juice of 1 fresh lime

¼ teaspoon ground cumin

⅛ teaspoon ground nutmeg

Salt and freshly ground white pepper to taste

4 tablespoons sour cream for garnish

1. In a large pot, over medium-high heat, sauté the shallots, apples, and squash in the butter. Then add the rest of the ingredients except the sour cream. Purée the soup, bring to a boil, and serve hot or cold. Garnish with sour cream.

FRESH SPRING SOUP WITH BABY PEAS

SERVES 4 | Calories: 292 | Protein: 4 grams | Carbohydrates: 28 grams | Fiber: 3 grams | Fat: 19 grams | Sodium: 740 milligrams

1 cup chopped spring onions or scallions

2 cloves garlic, smashed

1 bunch sorrel (or 1 bunch watercress)

10 young dandelion greens (small leaves only)

¼ cup olive oil

2 ounces arrowroot

3 cups GF Homemade Vegetable Stock (see recipe in Sauces, Stocks, and Special Additions)

⅛ teaspoon ground allspice

Zest of ½ lemon, minced

1½ cups fresh baby peas or 1 (10-ounce) package of frozen peas

1 cup soy cream

Salt and pepper to taste

1. Sauté the onions or scallions, the garlic, and the sorrel and dandelion greens in olive oil for 5 minutes, to wilt them.

2. Whisk in the arrowroot and vegetable stock. Stir in the allspice and lemon zest. When smooth, purée in the processor. Return the soup to the pot and add the peas. Cook for 5–8 minutes, or until tender.

3. Add the cream, salt, and pepper. Do not boil, but serve hot.

FRENCH GARLIC SOUP

SERVES 4 | Calories: 182 | Protein: 4 grams | Carbohydrates: 25 grams | Fiber: 4 grams | Fat: 7 grams | Sodium: 395 milligrams

2 tablespoons soy butter

1 large yellow onion (sliced medium)

8 large garlic cloves (minced fine)

4 cups GF Homemade Chicken Stock (see recipe in Sauces, Stocks, and Special Additions)

3 slices GF rice bread (stale or lightly toasted)

Salt and pepper to taste

Fresh Gluten-Free Croutons (see recipe in Sauces, Stocks, and Special Additions)

1. Heat a medium saucepan to medium heat.

2. Add butter, onion, and garlic to the pan. Sauté and stir the mixture for 2 minutes.

3. Add the stock and raise the heat to medium high. When the stock comes to a boil, add the bread and stir until bread is completely soaked.

4. Using a hand or immersion blender, blend the mixture until smooth. Reduce the heat to a simmer and continue to cook for 15 minutes.

5. Season with salt and pepper. Ladle the soup into a bowl, top with croutons, and serve.

LENTIL AND MUSHROOM SOUP

SERVES 4 | Calories: 375 | Protein: 15 grams | Carbohydrates: 38 grams | Fiber: 13 grams | Fat: 1 gram | Sodium: 668 milligrams

1 12-ounce bag lentils

Salt and pepper to taste

2 tablespoons olive oil

4 tablespoons soy butter

1 cup celery (chopped fine)

1 cup carrots (chopped fine)

1 cup white onions (chopped fine)

1 tablespoon cumin (ground)

4 cups GF Homemade Vegetable Stock (see recipe in Sauces, Stocks, and Special Additions)

2 tablespoons canola oil

6 medium white button mushrooms (rinsed, chopped medium)

1 cup cilantro (chopped fine)

1. Add the lentils, salt, and pepper to a small-sized soup pot. Pour in water until lentils are an inch underwater.

2. Bring the lentils to a boil, then add the olive oil, cover the pot, and reduce heat to simmer.

3. Cook for 20 minutes and set aside.

4. Heat a medium-sized soup pot to medium-high heat.

5. Add butter, celery, carrots, onions, cumin, salt, and pepper.

6. Sauté about 3 minutes or until the vegetables are softened.

7. Add the stock and stir well. Bring to a boil, then reduce the heat to low.

8. Heat a small sauté pan to medium-high heat. Add the canola oil and mushrooms to the pan.

9. Sauté the mushrooms until they just start to brown, then set aside.

10. Add the lentils and cilantro to the soup pot and stir to combine.

11. With a hand blender, blend until completely smooth. Add the mushrooms, stir, and divide soup evenly into 4 bowls. Serve.

GET THE **EDGE**

The fiber in this hearty and healthy soup will satisfy your hunger and keep you from overeating. Lentils contain mostly soluble fiber. Research indicates that soluble fiber may help to lower LDL cholesterol by attaching to the cholesterol particles and carrying them out of the body.

ROASTED CORN SOUP

SERVES 4 | Calories: 324 | Protein: 2 grams | Carbohydrates: 26 grams | Fiber: 2 grams | Fat: 24 grams | Sodium: 816 milligrams

3 ears corn (fresh, on the cob, shucked)

2 tablespoons canola oil

4 tablespoons soy butter

1 cup yellow onion

1 tablespoon cumin (ground)

Salt and pepper to taste

4 cups GF Homemade Vegetable Stock (see recipe in Sauces, Stocks, and Special Additions)

1 cup soy cream

2 tablespoons cornmeal

4 sprigs of cilantro

1. Heat grill to medium-high heat or set oven to broil.

2. With a paper towel, wipe each ear of corn with canola oil and place on the grill or under the broiler. Roast until browned on both sides and remove from the heat. When cooled, cut off all the corn kernels and set aside.

3. Meanwhile, heat a medium-sized soup pot to medium-high heat. Add butter, onions, cumin, salt, and pepper to the pan. Cook mixture until onions become opaque. Then add the stock and corn to the pot.

4. Bring the soup to a boil, then reduce heat and simmer for 5 minutes.

5. Add the cream to the pot and purée the soup with a hand blender for 2 minutes or until completely blended together.

6. Ladle into soup bowls and sprinkle with cornmeal. Garnish each bowl with a sprig of cilantro and serve.

BAJA CHICKEN NOODLE SOUP

SERVES 4 | Calories: 425 | Protein: 18 grams | Carbohydrates: 42 grams | Fiber: 6 grams | Fat: 21 grams | Sodium: 291 milligrams

3 tablespoons canola oil

1 carrot (cut into ¼" disks)

1 rib celery (cut into ¼" slices)

1 small yellow onion (peeled, halved, cut into ¼" slices)

2 garlic cloves (minced fine)

1 tablespoon oregano (dried)

Cracked black pepper to taste

4 cups GF Homemade Chicken Stock (see recipe in Sauces, Stocks, and Special Additions)

1 lime (juiced and zested)

1 tablespoon lime zest

1 8-ounce chicken breast (boneless, skinless, cooked, rough chopped)

2 cups GF corn tortilla strips

1. Heat a medium-size soup pot to medium-high heat.

2. Add and heat the oil for 10 seconds, then add the carrot, celery, onion, garlic, oregano, and pepper.

3. Stirring often, cook about 4 minutes until onions become transparent. Reduce heat to medium and add the stock, lime juice, lime zest, and chicken.

4. Bring to a boil and reduce heat to low. Let the soup simmer for 15 minutes.

5. Add the tortilla strips and stir, then ladle an even amount into 4 soup bowls and serve.

BROCCOLI SOUP

SERVES 4 | Calories: 295 | Protein: 5 grams | Carbohydrates: 30 grams | Fiber: 3 grams | Fat: 18 grams | Sodium: 428 milligrams

4 tablespoons soy butter

4 cups broccoli florets (fresh only!)

3 shallots (chopped fine)

1 carrot (chopped small)

Salt and pepper to taste

1 garlic clove (minced fine)

4 cups GF Homemade Vegetable Stock (see recipe in Sauces, Stocks, and Special Additions)

1 cup soy cream

1 tablespoon arrowroot (dissolved in a small cup with 2 tablespoons of room-temperature water)

Fresh Gluten-Free Croutons (for garnish) (see recipe in Sauces, Stocks, and Special Additions)

1. Heat a medium-size soup pot to medium-high heat. Add butter and heat for 10 seconds, then add the broccoli, shallots, carrot, salt, pepper, and garlic to the pot.

2. Cook for 5 minutes while stirring with a wooden spoon to release the flavors.

3. Add the stock and stir to combine.

4. Bring heat down to a simmer and cook for 15 minutes.

5. With a hand blender, purée the soup until smooth.

6. Add the cream and arrowroot and blend the soup again.

7. Ladle evenly into 4 soup bowls, garnish with croutons, and serve.

FRENCH ONION SOUP

SERVES 4 | Calories: 383 | Protein: 18 grams | Carbohydrates: 17 grams | Fiber: 2 grams | Fat: 25 grams | Sodium: 975 milligrams

2 tablespoons olive oil

3 medium yellow onions (peeled, halved then sliced thin)

2 tablespoons fresh thyme leaves

1 shallot (chopped small)

Salt and pepper to taste

4 slices GF bread (cut into ½" slices)

2 tablespoons sherry

2 tablespoons white wine

4 cups GF Homemade Vegetable Stock (see recipe in Sauces, Stocks, and Special Additions)

2 cups Gruyère cheese

1. Preheat oven to 400°F.

2. Heat a medium-sized soup pot to medium-high heat. Add the oil and heat for 10 seconds. Then add the onions, thyme, shallot, salt, and pepper and cook for 3 minutes.

3. Add the sherry and white wine and reduce heat to medium. After 1 minute, add the stock and bring to a boil. Reduce heat to low and cook for 20 minutes to release all the flavors.

4. Meanwhile, with a ring cutter or drinking glass, cut the bread slices into disks that match the circumference of the crocks.

5. Ladle the soup into 4 soup crocks, leaving an inch at the top.

6. Add a disk to each crock and cover with a generous helping of Gruyère cheese.

7. Place the crocks on a baking sheet and cook for 10 minutes. Serve.

NEW ENGLAND CLAM CHOWDER

SERVES 4 | Calories: 431 | Protein: 31 grams | Carbohydrates: 29 grams | Fiber: 1 gram | Fat: 20 grams | Sodium: 756 milligrams

4 tablespoons soy butter

1 white onion (chopped medium)

1 celery rib (cut into ¼" slices)

2 garlic cloves (minced fine)

2 cups GF Homemade Vegetable Stock (see recipe in Sauces, Stocks, and Special Additions)

1 large russet potato (peeled, cut into ½" cubes)

Salt and pepper to taste

2 bay leaves

2 cans chopped clams (reserve liquid)

1 cup soy cream

1 tablespoon arrowroot (mix with 1 tablespoon water in a small cup)

Fresh Gluten-Free Croutons (for garnish) (see recipe in Sauces, Stocks, and Special Additions)

1. Heat a medium-sized soup pot to medium-high heat.

2. Add the butter to the pot, heat for 10 seconds, then add the onion, celery, and garlic. Cook for 2 minutes and then add the stock, potatoes, salt, pepper, bay leaves, and clams (with liquid).

3. Stir mixture until combined. Cover pot, reduce heat to low, and cook for 15 minutes.

4. Add the cream and the arrowroot mixture and gently stir until the soup begins to thicken.

5. Cook for 5 minutes, ladle into 4 soup bowls, garnish with croutons, and serve.

WHITE BEAN MINESTRONE

SERVES 4 | Calories: 402 | Protein: 13 grams | Carbohydrates: 55 grams | Fiber: 9 grams | Fat: 15 grams | Sodium: 1060 milligrams

1 15-ounce can cannellini white beans

1 medium zucchini (diced small)

3 tablespoons olive oil

1 large carrot (diced small)

1 yellow onion (chopped medium)

1 celery rib (⅛" slices)

3 garlic cloves (rough chopped)

3 Roma tomatoes (diced small)

1 tablespoon tomato paste

4 thyme sprigs (leaves removed)

Salt and pepper to taste

4 cups GF Homemade Vegetable Stock
(see recipe in Sauces, Stocks, and Special
Additions)

2 cups rice pasta elbows

2 bay leaves

4 tablespoons Parmigiano-Reggiano
cheese (sliced thin for garnish)

1. Heat a medium-sized soup pot to medium-high heat. Add the oil and heat for 10 seconds, then add the carrot, onion, celery, and garlic. Cook for 3 minutes, then reduce the heat to medium.

2. Add the tomatoes, tomato paste, thyme, salt, and pepper and stir the mixture with a wooden spoon to combine.

3. Add the stock, pasta, beans, zucchini, and bay leaves and bring to a boil. Then reduce the heat to low. Let sit for 20 minutes.

4. Remove the bay leaves then ladle into 4 soup bowls, garnish with Parmigiano-Reggiano cheese, and serve.

GET THE **EDGE**

Minestrone soup is a traditional peasant food that is hearty and delicious. Here we've substituted rice pasta for the semolina pasta that is typically used in the recipe. This soup is loaded with vitamins and minerals such as vitamins A, C, B6, and potassium. It can be eaten as a meal or served as a side.

SPLIT PEA AND TURKEY SOUP

SERVES 4 | Calories: 380 | Protein: 27 grams | Carbohydrates: 32 grams | Fiber: 10 grams |
Fat: 16 grams | Sodium: 611 milligrams

2 tablespoons olive oil

1 cup yellow onion (chopped fine)

1 cup carrots (chopped fine)

1 cup celery (chopped fine)

4 cups GF Homemade Vegetable Stock
(see recipe in Sauces, Stocks, and Special
Additions)

1 pound split peas

Salt and pepper to taste

1 cup soy milk

1 cup cooked turkey (chopped fine)

1. Heat a medium-sized soup pot to medium-high heat. Add the olive oil, heat for 30 seconds, then add the onions, carrots, and celery.

2. Cook for 3 minutes or until the vegetables are softened.

3. Add the stock, peas, salt, and pepper. Bring to a boil and reduce heat to a simmer. Cook for 45 minutes.

4. Add the milk to the pot, then blend until smooth with a hand blender.

5. Add the turkey to the pot and stir until blended. Ladle evenly into 4 soup bowls and serve.

CRISPY RICE AND CHICKEN SOUP

SERVES 4 | Calories: 538 | Protein: 33 grams | Carbohydrates: 35 grams | Fiber: 4 grams | Fat: 30 grams | Sodium: 1331 milligrams

4 cups Homemade GF Chicken Stock (see recipe in Sauces, Stocks, and Special Additions)

½ cup canola oil

2 8-ounce chicken breasts (boneless, skinless)

1 cup baby ears of corn (halved the wide way)

1 cup green onions (topped, cut into thin slices on the bias)

1 cup snow peas

2 garlic cloves (minced fine)

½ cup tamari

1 teaspoon white pepper

2 cups bean sprouts

8 cilantro sprigs (4 chopped fine, 4 for garnish)

2 cups long grain rice (cooked)

1. Heat a large-size soup pot to medium-high heat. Add ½ the canola oil and heat for 20 seconds, then add the chicken breasts. Sear the chicken on both sides for about 1 minute per side. Remove the chicken and let cool for 2 minutes.

2. Cut the chicken into 1" cubes and return to the pot. Add stock and bring to a boil. Reduce heat to low, add the corn, onions, peas, garlic, tamari, and pepper, and cover. Cook for 10 minutes and add the sprouts and chopped cilantro to the pot. Cook for 5–7 more minutes and divide evenly into 4 soup bowls.

3. Heat a medium-size sauté pan to medium-high heat for 20 seconds. Add the other ½ of the oil and the cooked rice. With a spatula, flatten the rice as tightly as possible to make "pancake"-shaped cakes. Brown the rice on both sides and, when it's very hot, place it on a paper towel–covered plate and pat the oil dry on both sides quickly. Remove the paper towels, break up the "pancake" into about 8 pieces, and drop into the soup pot. Ladle into 4 bowls, garnish with a cilantro sprig and serve.

FAVA BEAN AND BABY CARROT SOUP

SERVES 4 | Calories: 153 | Protein: 10 grams | Carbohydrates: 20 grams | Fiber: 1 gram | Fat: 5 grams | Sodium: 124 milligrams

1 cup fresh leek (white part only, cut into ¼" slices)

12 baby carrots (peeled, top trimmed to 1")

Sea salt and pepper to taste

4½ cups GF Homemade Chicken Stock (see recipe in Sauces, Stocks, and Special Additions)

2 cups fresh fava beans (shelled)

1 tablespoon canola oil

1. Heat a large saucepan over medium heat and after 20 seconds add the oil

2. Add leeks, carrots, salt, and pepper and sauté for 8 minutes or until vegetables are tender but not brown. Add stock and bring to boil. Add fava beans and simmer until almost tender or about 8 minutes. Simmer until all vegetables are very tender, about 7 minutes longer. Ladle the soup into 4 bowls and serve.

FENNEL AND CHICKEN SOUP

SERVES 4 | Calories: 280 | Protein: 32 grams | Carbohydrates: 10 grams | Fiber: 2 grams | Fat: 13 grams | Sodium: 489 milligrams

2 tablespoons canola oil

2 8-ounce chicken breasts (boneless, skinless, salt and peppered to taste)

1 large bulb fennel (without leaves or stems; save 4 fronds for garnish)

Salt and pepper to taste

4 cups GF Homemade Chicken Stock (see recipe in Sauces, Stocks, and Special Additions)

½ cup soy cream

1. Heat a large soup pot to medium heat for 20 seconds. Add the oil and the chicken breasts and sear the chicken on each side for 1 minute. Set chicken aside to cool.

2. Cut fennel into quarters lengthwise and remove hard core. Slice into ⅛" strips.

3. Add stock to the pot and bring to a boil. Add fennel, salt, and pepper. Cook the soup until the fennel is tender, or about 15 to 20 minutes.

4. Cut the chicken into 1" cubes and add it and the cream to the soup and simmer for 5 more minutes. Divide the soup evenly into 4 bowls, garnish with a fennel frond, and serve.

ITALIAN TOMATO AND SHRIMP SOUP

SERVES 4 | Calories: 205 | Protein: 15 grams | Carbohydrates: 21 grams | Fiber: 4 grams | Fat: 8 grams | Sodium: 1108 milligrams

2 tablespoons olive oil

2 tablespoons oregano (dried)

2 tablespoons fresh basil (chopped fine)

Salt and pepper to taste

½ pound medium shrimp (peeled, deveined, tails off; save 4 for garnish)

1 medium onion (chopped medium)

2 cups zucchini (medium dice)

1 28-ounce can San Marzano peeled tomatoes (chopped medium)

4 cups GF Homemade Vegetable Stock (see recipe in Sauces, Stocks, and Special Additions)

1. Heat a large soup pot to medium heat for 20 seconds. Add the olive oil, herbs, shrimp, onion, salt, and pepper to the pot. Sauté the onions until they become opaque. Remove 4 of the shrimp for garnish. Then proceed to add the zucchini and tomatoes to the pot. Cook the mixture for 2 minutes and add the stock to the pot. Bring the soup to a boil and lower the heat to a simmer. Cook the soup for 5 minutes, divide evenly into 4 soup bowls, garnish with a butterflied shrimp on top, and serve.

WILD, WILD RICE AND MUSHROOM SOUP

MAKES 6 CUPS | Calories: 264 | Protein: 6 grams | Carbohydrates: 33 grams | Fiber: 2 grams | Fat: 10 grams | Sodium: 505 milligrams

3 tablespoons butter

2 cloves garlic, minced

1 cup finely chopped sweet onion such as Vidalia

10 each: shiitake, morel, porcini, and oyster mushrooms, brushed clean and chopped

2 tablespoons arrowroot

5 cups GF Homemade Vegetable Stock (see recipe in Sauces, Stocks, and Special Additions)

2 cups cooked wild rice

1 cup soy cream

Salt and pepper to taste

½ cup dry sherry

6 fresh sage leaves

1. Melt the butter and add the garlic and onion. Sauté for 5 minutes and add the mushrooms. Add the arrowroot and stir until thickened, cooking for another 5 minutes.

2. Slowly stir in the stock, stirring constantly. Mix in the wild rice. Add the cream, salt, and pepper.

3. Add the sherry and serve in heated bowls, with a sage leaf floating in each one.

GET THE **EDGE**

This versatile soup can be an elegant first course for company, or it can be served with gluten-free bread and a salad as a light supper.

SHRIMP AND COCONUT SOUP

SERVES 4 | Calories: 334 | Protein: 26 grams | Carbohydrates: 17 grams | Fiber: <1 gram | Fat: 15 grams | Sodium: 551 milligrams

2 shallots, minced

2 teaspoons peanut oil or other vegetable oil

2 tablespoons arrowroot

1½ cups Shrimp Shell Broth (see recipe), warmed

½ cup dry white wine

1 cup unsweetened coconut milk

1 cup cooked rice (optional)

1 pound shrimp, shelled and deveined, chopped

Salt and freshly ground white pepper to taste

1. Add 1 cup of water, 1 cup of wine, and a bay leaf to the shells from a pound of shrimp. Bring to a boil, lower heat, and simmer, covered, for 20 minutes. Strain and set broth aside.

2. Sauté the shallots in the oil until soft, about 10 minutes over medium heat. Stir in the arrowroot and cook until very thick.

3. Add the liquid ingredients and cook, covered, over very low heat for 30 minutes.

4. Stir in the rice and shrimp; heat until the shrimp turns pink. Add salt and white pepper to taste and serve hot or cold.

GRILLED EGGPLANT AND PEPPER SALAD

SERVES 12 | Calories: 211 | Protein: 3 grams | Carbohydrates: 6 grams | Fiber: 2 grams | Fat: 20 grams | Sodium: 193 milligrams

½ cup canola oil

⅜ cup balsamic or red wine vinegar

1 cup olive oil

1 teaspoon Dijon-style mustard

Salt and pepper to taste

1 medium eggplant, peeled and sliced in ½ inch rounds

3 red bell peppers, cored and seeded, cut in half

1 bunch arugula or watercress, stems removed, washed

1 large head romaine lettuce, washed, dried, and chopped

4 ripe tomatoes, cored and chopped

2 ounces aged provolone cheese

1. Brush the grill with canola oil and heat to medium-high heat.

2. To prepare the dressing, mix the vinegar, olive oil, mustard, salt, and pepper together in a cruet. Shake well. Cut the eggplant into ½-inch slices, brush with the salad dressing, and grill for 3 minutes on each side. Cool and cut into cubes.

3. Grill the peppers on the skin side until charred. Place in a paper bag to steam the skin away from the pepper. Cool and pull the skin off. Cut into pieces.

4. Just before serving, toss the greens with the eggplant and peppers, add tomatoes, and shave the provolone over the top. Dress and serve.

BISTRO LENTIL SALAD

SERVES 6 | Calories: 334 | Protein: 9 grams | Carbohydrates: 21 grams | Fiber: 7 grams | Fat: 25 grams | Sodium: 235 milligrams

1 16-ounce package red lentils or small French lentils

2 cups GF Homemade Chicken Stock (see recipe in Sauces, Stocks, and Special Additions)

Water, as needed

2 garlic cloves, smashed and peeled

2 whole cloves

½ cup finely chopped sweet red onion

1 sweet red bell pepper, roasted, peeled, and chopped

2 stalks celery, washed and finely chopped

½ cup chopped fresh parsley

2 teaspoons dried oregano

1 teaspoon prepared Dijon mustard

2 tablespoons lemon juice

2 tablespoons red wine vinegar

⅔ cup extra-virgin olive oil

1. Combine the lentils and stock and add water to cover. Add the garlic and cloves. Bring the lentils to a boil and reduce heat to simmer. Cook until tender, about 20 minutes. Drain and place in a large serving bowl. Remove garlic and cloves.

2. Mix the rest of the ingredients with the lentils and chill for 2–3 hours. Just before serving, heat for a few seconds in the microwave. Or serve well chilled with shredded lettuce.

EL VAQUERO CHICKEN SALAD

SERVES 4 | Calories: 643 | Protein: 59 grams | Carbohydrates: 45 grams | Fiber: 10 grams | Fat: 25 grams | Sodium: 893 milligrams

4 tablespoons canola oil

Salt and pepper to taste

4 8-ounce medium boneless, skinless chicken breasts

1 head Romaine lettuce (chopped)

1½ cups cherry tomatoes (halved)

8 dates (rough chopped)

1 cup roasted red peppers (cut into 1"-length slices)

1 ripe avocado (cut into 1" cubes)

2 tablespoons lime juice

2 cups Fresh Gluten-Free Croutons (see recipe in Sauces, Stocks, and Special Additions)

1. Heat a medium-size sauté pan to medium-high heat.

2. Add canola oil to hot pan and heat until ripples appear in oil.

3. Salt and pepper chicken breasts and sauté for 3 minutes per side or until both sides are light golden brown and cooked through.

4. Remove chicken from pan and let rest for 5 minutes before chopping into bite-sized pieces.

5. Meanwhile, in a medium-size bowl, add the lettuce, tomatoes, dates, red peppers, avocado, and lime juice.

6. Add chicken and toss salad to blend in. Top with croutons, add your favorite dressing, and serve.

CHOPPED ROAST TURKEY SALAD

SERVES 4 | Calories: 559 | Protein: 25 grams | Carbohydrates: 58 grams | Fiber: 10 grams | Fat: 27 grams | Sodium: 809 milligrams

1 head romaine lettuce (chopped)

2 cups cherry tomatoes (halved)

1 cup red onion (chopped fine)

1 cup dried cranberries (rough chopped)

1 ripe avocado (cut into ½" cubes)

1 cup fresh cilantro (cut into 1"-length slices)

16 ounces roasted turkey breast (chopped medium)

4 tablespoons olive oil

3 tablespoons white balsamic vinegar

Salt and pepper to taste

2 cups Fresh Gluten-Free Croutons (see recipe in Sauces, Stocks, and Special Additions)

1. In a medium-sized bowl, add the lettuce, tomatoes, onion, cranberries, avocado, and cilantro.

2. Add turkey and toss salad to blend.

3. In a small bowl add the olive oil and vinegar and whisk until blended. Salt and pepper the dressing to taste, add to the salad, and toss. Top with croutons and serve.

GET THE EDGE

When buying turkey at your local grocery store, low sodium, organic turkey is your best choice. If you buy pre-sliced turkey be sure they slice it with a clean knife to avoid possible cross-contamination from gluten. It is always best to avoid turkey that has been sliced and pre-packaged.

FOUR-BEAN SALAD

SERVES 4 | Calories: 374 | Protein: 9 grams | Carbohydrates: 32 grams | Fiber: 8 grams |
Fat: 24 grams | Sodium: 305 milligrams

2 cups red kidney beans (drained)

2 cups yellow wax beans (drained)

2 cups garbanzo beans (drained)

2 cups white beans (drained)

1 cup white onion (sliced paper-thin)

1 cup canola oil

½ cup white balsamic vinegar

2 tablespoons dried oregano

Salt and cracked black pepper

1. In a medium-size mixing bowl, add all ingredients and stir gently until blended together.

2. Let stand for 20–30 minutes to allow ingredients to marinate, and serve.

SWEET POTATO SALAD

SERVES 4 | Calories: 432 | Protein: 3 grams | Carbohydrates: 32 grams | Fiber: 5 grams | Fat: 35 grams | Sodium: 37 milligrams

4 tablespoons unsalted butter

1 pound sweet potatoes (peeled and cut into 1" cubes)

1 head romaine lettuce (rough chopped)

1 cup red onion (chopped fine)

1 cup fresh or canned pineapple (rough chopped or small pieces)

1 cup fresh cilantro (rough chopped)

2 cups Roma tomatoes (rough chopped)

1 teaspoon fresh nutmeg

1 teaspoon cinnamon

1 cup canola oil

½ cup white balsamic vinegar

Salt and pepper to taste

1. Heat a medium saucepan to medium-high heat. Add butter and potatoes and then add enough water to cover the potatoes with an extra inch of water above. Bring the potatoes to a boil and reduce heat to medium.

2. Cook potatoes for 25 minutes or until tender; drain. Place potatoes in a medium-size bowl and refrigerate for about 15 minutes or until cool.

3. Once potatoes are cool, add lettuce, onion, pineapple, cilantro, tomatoes, nutmeg, and cinnamon, and combine.

4. In a small bowl add the oil and vinegar and whisk until blended. Salt and pepper the dressing, add to the salad, toss, and serve.

GET THE **EDGE**

Many people on a gluten-free diet crave bread and other grains because they're filling. The sweet potato is a perfect replacement for that craving for grains to fill you up. In addition, sweet potatoes are low in saturated fat and provide a good source of potassium and vitamin B6.

CHOPPED LOX SALAD

SERVES 4 | Calories: 303 | Protein: 29 grams | Carbohydrates: 24 grams | Fiber: 2 grams | Fat: 9 grams | Sodium: 1313 milligrams

16 ounces lox (smoked salmon), rough chopped

1 head Boston butter lettuce (hand-torn)

1 cup red onion (chopped small)

2 cups Roma tomatoes (chopped medium)

4 tablespoons capers

Cracked black pepper to taste

3 hard-boiled eggs (rough chopped)

2 cups GF bagel chips

1. Combine lox, lettuce, onion, tomatoes, capers, and pepper, and toss lightly with vinaigrette of choice.

2. Garnish with egg and bagel chips and serve.

CHOPPED CHICKEN AND BEET SALAD

SERVES 4 | Calories: 654 | Protein: 36 grams | Carbohydrates: 22 grams | Fiber: 7 grams | Fat: 57 grams | Sodium: 205 milligrams

1 cup canola oil plus 2 tablespoons (for sautéing chicken)

2 8-ounce chicken breasts (boneless, skinless)

Celery salt and black pepper to taste

1 cup red onion (sliced thin)

2 cups red cabbage (shredded)

1 head romaine lettuce (chopped small)

1 celery rib (cut into ¼" slices)

1 15-ounce can red beets (sliced, not pickled)

1 cup cherry tomatoes (halved)

½ cup white balsamic vinegar

1 tablespoon apple cider vinegar

Celery salt and cracked black pepper to taste

1. Heat a medium-sized sauté pan to medium heat. Add 2 tablespoons of oil to the pan and heat for 20 seconds.

2. Season chicken with celery salt and pepper. Add to the pan and cook for 2 minutes on each side to sear in the juices. Add the red onion and cabbage, cover the pan, and cook for 5 minutes or until cooked through, then set aside to let cool.

3. Chop the chicken up into small dice using a large kitchen knife, and add to sautéed mixture.

4. In a large salad bowl, add the lettuce, celery, beets, and tomatoes and toss to combine.

5. In a small mixing bowl, add remaining cup of oil, both vinegars, salt, and pepper. With a small whisk, rapidly stir the mixture together until blended well. Pour the dressing over the salad and then toss gently to coat the salad evenly.

6. Divide the salad evenly onto 4 plates, spoon a generous amount of the chicken mixture on top of each, and serve.

GET THE **EDGE**

When shopping for beets you want to find beets that are small, firm, well-rounded, and uniformly sized. Beets with bright, crisp greens on top are the freshest. The skins should be smooth and deep red.

CRISPY RICE ASIAN SALAD

SERVES 4 | Calories: 807 | Protein: 10 grams | Carbohydrates: 63 grams | Fiber: 10 grams | Fat: 60 grams | Sodium: 164 milligrams

1 cup canola oil plus 3 tablespoons for frying the rice

2 cups long grain brown rice (cooked, well drained)

1 head romaine lettuce (small chopped)

1 15-ounce can mandarin oranges (drain the juice into a small mixing bowl and reserve)

2 cups bean sprouts

1 15-ounce can baby ears of corn (cut into 1" pieces)

2 cups snow peas

4 green onions (chopped small)

1 cup cilantro (chopped fine)

1 tablespoon toasted sesame oil

4 tablespoons Mirin rice wine vinegar

Salt and pepper to taste

1. Heat a medium-size sauté pan to medium-high heat. Add 3 tablespoons of canola oil to the pan and heat for 1 minute. Add the cooked rice to the hot pan and proceed to pack the rice down tightly, with a spatula, around the entire bottom of the pan as to form a large, thin rice cake. Cook for 3 minutes on each side or until browned and crispy. Remove from heat and set aside.

2. Combine the lettuce, oranges, sprouts, corn, peas, onions, and cilantro in a large salad bowl.

3. In a small mixing bowl add the remaining cup of canola oil, sesame oil, vinegar, reserved orange liquid, salt, and pepper. Whisk for 1 minute and dress the salad.

4. Break the rice cake into small pieces and sprinkle on top of the salad, then gently toss. Divide onto 4 plates and serve.

CURRIED BAY SHRIMP AND BROCCOLI SALAD

SERVES 4 | Calories: 735 | Protein: 29 grams | Carbohydrates: 21 grams | Fiber: 5 grams | Fat: 61 grams | Sodium: 335 milligrams

2 tablespoons yellow curry powder

1 cup soy cream

Salt and pepper to taste

1 pound precooked bay shrimp (rinsed, drained well)

4 cups broccoli florets (chopped small)

1 head romaine lettuce (chopped small)

2 cups cherry tomatoes

1 cup flat-leaf parsley (rough chopped), plus 1 cup for garnish

1 cup olive oil

½ cup white balsamic vinegar

1. In a small mixing bowl combine the curry powder, cream, salt, and pepper, then add the shrimp and gently coat thoroughly.

2. In a large salad bowl, combine the broccoli, lettuce, tomatoes, and parsley.

3. In a small mixing bowl, add the oil, vinegar, salt, and pepper. Whisk rapidly to make a smooth dressing.

4. Pour the dressing over the salad in the salad bowl and toss well.

5. Divide the salad onto 4 plates, top each salad with a generous amount of the shrimp curry mixture, garnish with parsley, and serve.

GRAPEFRUIT AND AVOCADO SALAD

SERVES 4 | Calories: 524 | Protein: 9 grams | Carbohydrates: 69 grams | Fiber: 13 grams | Fat: 26 grams | Sodium: 468 milligrams

2 grapefruits (peeled and sections separated)

1 head romaine lettuce (chopped small)

1 cup red onion (chopped small)

1 cup black olives (pitted, medium)

1 large avocado (ripe, cut into 1" cubes)

1 cup cherry tomatoes

1 cup cilantro (chopped small)

1 tablespoon cumin (ground)

2 tablespoons canola oil

2 tablespoons lime juice

Salt and cracked black pepper to taste

2 cups blue corn tortillas (crumbled)

1. In a large salad bowl, add the grapefruit, lettuce, onions, olives, avocado, tomatoes, cumin, and cilantro. With 2 large wooden spoons, gently toss the salad to incorporate the ingredients.

2. In a small mixing bowl, add the canola oil, lime juice, salt, and pepper and whisk to combine.

3. Add the crumbled blue corn tortillas over the top of the salad, gently toss to combine, then divide the salad evenly onto 4 plates and serve.

GET THE **EDGE**

Studies have shown that grapefruit may actually block enzymes involved in fat and carbohydrate storage, and speed up the way your body burns fat—all of which results in weight loss. Grapefruit is low in calories and low in sodium, and definitely is an excellent food to eat anytime, so feel free to eat up. However, citrus fruits can interfere with certain medications so consult with your doctor before eating.

GRILLED PORTOBELLO MUSHROOM, RED ONION, AND ZUCCHINI SALAD

SERVES 4 | Calories: 244 | Protein: 4 grams | Carbohydrates: 13 grams | Fiber: 6 grams | Fat: 21 grams | Sodium: 162 milligrams

2 portobello mushrooms (stem removed, scraped clean under top)

1 medium red onion (peeled, cut into ½" slices)

1 large zucchini (quartered lengthwise)

2 tablespoons canola oil

1 head romaine lettuce (chopped small)

2 cups cherry tomatoes

1 cup fresh basil leaves (stacked, rolled, then sliced thin into ⅛" thin ribbons)

1 tablespoon oregano

Salt and pepper to taste

2 tablespoons balsamic vinegar

4 tablespoons olive oil

1. Heat your outdoor or indoor grill to medium heat.

2. With a paper towel or brush, coat the mushrooms, onion, and zucchini with canola oil, then place the vegetables on the grill and cook for 2 minutes per side. Then turn them again for another 2 minutes to get the crossed grill marks on the vegetables, remove from heat, and set aside.

3. In a large salad bowl combine the lettuce, tomatoes, basil, oregano, salt, and pepper.

4. When cooled, slice the mushrooms, separate the rings of the onion, and add all the vegetables to the salad bowl.

5. Add the balsamic vinegar to a small mixing bowl, then stream in the olive oil while whisking to combine the two ingredients. When completely combined, add salt and pepper and whisk to combine.

6. Pour the dressing over the salad and toss well to coat the vegetables and the lettuce. Divide the salad evenly into 4 salad bowls and serve.

GET THE **EDGE**

Portobello mushrooms are similar in texture and flavor to several types of beef, which is usually loaded with saturated fat and carcinogens. Incorporate these mushrooms into any recipe you currently make with beef and make weight loss your main priority.

ROASTED ARTICHOKE AND VEGETABLE SALAD

SERVES 4 | Calories: 686 | Protein: 9 grams | Carbohydrates: 26 grams | Fiber: 12 grams | Fat: 53 grams | Sodium: 411 milligrams

2 15-ounce jars/cans marinated artichoke hearts (drained well)

1 red bell pepper (cleaned, cut into 1"-wide strips)

2 cups red onion (cut into ½" slices)

1 large carrot (peeled, cut into ½" disks)

4 tablespoons canola oil

Salt and cracked black pepper to taste

1 head romaine lettuce (chopped medium)

2 cups red heirloom tomatoes (cut into ½" wedges)

½ cup white balsamic vinegar

1 cup olive oil

2 cups Fresh Gluten-Free Croutons (for garnish) (see recipe in Sauces, Stocks, and Special Additions)

1. Preheat oven to 350°F.

2. Combine artichokes, red pepper, onion, carrot, canola oil, salt, and pepper in a large salad bowl. With 2 large wooden spoons, toss the vegetables to coat them with the oil.

3. Spread the vegetables out evenly on a foil-lined baking sheet. Cook for 20 minutes. Remove from oven and let cool for 5 minutes.

4. Meanwhile, combine lettuce and tomato in the same salad bowl.

5. Add balsamic vinegar to a small mixing bowl. With a whisk in one hand, stream the olive oil into the bowl and whisk vigorously to combine. Add salt and pepper and whisk to thoroughly combine. Set aside.

6. Add the roasted vegetables to the bowl.

7. Pour the vinaigrette over the top of the salad and gently toss until vegetables are coated with the dressing.

8. Divide evenly onto 4 plates, garnish with croutons, and serve.

ROASTED GREEN BELL PEPPER AND GARBANZO BEAN SALAD

SERVES 4 | Calories: 902 | Protein: 19 grams | Carbohydrates: 45 grams | Fiber: 11 grams | Fat: 74 grams | Sodium: 1621 milligrams

1 green bell pepper (cut down each of the 4 sides into 4 large pieces, brush with canola oil)

1 head romaine lettuce (chopped small)

1 cup extra-virgin olive oil

4 tablespoons white balsamic vinegar

2 tablespoons lemon juice

Salt and pepper to taste

½ cup mint (chopped small)

2 cups garbanzo beans (drained and rinsed)

2 tablespoons oregano

2 Roma tomatoes (cut into ½" dice)

1 red onion (halved, ¼" slices separated into half rings)

1 cup black olives

2 cups crumbled feta cheese

1. Heat your oven to broil. Place the peppers under the broiler and cook until charred on both sides, then remove to a small plate and set aside to cool. Once cool, slice the peppers into ¼" lengths and set aside.

2. In a large salad bowl add the lettuce, then add the olive oil, vinegar, lemon juice, salt, and pepper. Toss, using 2 large wooden spoons, for 30 seconds.

3. Add the remaining vegetables, mint, oregano, and cheese, then gently toss all the ingredients together for 10 seconds. Divide the salad evenly onto 4 plates and serve.

GET THE **EDGE**

This is a simple, easy-to-make side dish that is packed with surprising flavor and nutritional value. The pepper contains vitamin C and the beans are a great source of vegetarian protein. This side works well with most of the Entrées in this book, but it's best to eat with a vegetarian meal because the garbanzo beans are loaded with the extra protein that you'll need to fill you up.

SEA SCALLOPS AND ROASTED CORN SALAD

SERVES 4 | Calories: 390 | Protein: 36 grams | Carbohydrates: 13 grams | Fiber: 6 grams | Fat: 22 grams | Sodium: 482 milligrams

2 tablespoons canola oil plus extra to wipe down the grill

1½ pounds sea scallops (cut into small dice)

2 tablespoons paprika

2 tablespoons cumin (ground)

Salt and pepper to taste

4 tablespoons soy butter (melted in small dish)

1 ear fresh corn (not frozen or canned)

1 medium red bell pepper (4 sides cut into 4 large pieces)

1 head romaine lettuce (chopped small)

1 cup fresh cilantro (chopped small) plus 4 sprigs for garnish

2 tablespoons lime juice

1. Heat your indoor or outdoor grill to medium-high heat. While it's starting to come to heat, wipe the grill with canola oil on a paper towel to coat the grill.

2. Lay out the scallops on a large plate and season with paprika, cumin, salt, and pepper.

3. Dip each scallop in the melted butter and place on the grill. Cook for 1 minute or until lightly browned on each side and then remove from the grill back to the plate. Cover the scallops with foil and set aside.

4. Coat the corn and red pepper with some of the canola oil and then place on grill. Reserve the rest of the canola oil for dressing. Cook both vegetables for 3 minutes or until the pepper slices are charred and the corn is gently browned. Remove from the grill and set aside to cool.

5. In a large salad bowl, combine the lettuce, cilantro, reserved canola oil, and lime juice. Toss to coat the lettuce.

6. Cut the cooled scallops into small dice and add to the salad.

7. Trim all the corn kernels off the cob with a sharp knife into a bowl and add them to the salad. Slice the red peppers into ¼"-wide slices, add to the salad bowl, and gently toss with wooden spoons.

8. Divide the salad evenly onto 4 plates, garnish with a cilantro sprig, and serve.

GET THE EDGE

Instead of a bowl of clam chowder, try this scrumptious salad for a light start to a beautiful dinner. The raw vegetables in the salad provide plenty of nutritional value without making you feel too full for your entrée. Studies show that eating plenty of raw vegetables helps speed up weight loss and prevents gaining back weight once it is lost. In addition, sea scallops are rich in omega-3 fats, which improve cardiovascular health.

GRILLED SHRIMP SALAD

SERVES 4 | Calories: 420 | Protein: 28 grams | Carbohydrates: 24 grams | Fiber: 8 grams | Fat: 24 grams | Sodium: 284 milligrams

4 wooden skewers

2 yellow or red bell peppers (cleaned)

1 red onion

1 pound uncooked medium (31–40 size) shrimp (peeled, deveined, tail on)

3 tablespoons paprika

2 tablespoons onion powder

Salt and cracked pepper to taste

8 tablespoons unsalted butter

1 head romaine lettuce (rough chopped)

2 cups cherry tomatoes (halved)

Vinaigrette dressing of your choice

1 lemon (cut into wedges, pits removed)

1. Soak the wooden skewers in water for 20 minutes.

2. Meanwhile, heat an indoor or outdoor grill to medium-high heat.

3. Cut the bell peppers and red onion into 1½" squares.

4. Sprinkle the shrimp with paprika, onion powder, salt, and cracked pepper.

5. Assemble skewers by sliding on a bell pepper square, then an onion square, then 3 shrimp; repeat until each skewer is filled. Make sure to spear the shrimp through the meatiest part near the head.

6. Melt butter in small cup and brush shrimp generously. Grill the shrimp skewer until all the shrimp are pink.

7. Place the lettuce and tomatoes in a medium-sized bowl and toss with a vinaigrette dressing of your choice. Remove the lettuce and tomatoes to a platter and place the shrimp skewers on top. Garnish with a couple of lemon wedges, then serve.

TOASTED SESAME AND GARLIC CAULIFLOWER SALAD

SERVES 4 | Calories: 613 | Protein: 6 grams | Carbohydrates: 15 grams | Fiber: 7 grams | Fat: 61 grams | Sodium: 1179 milligrams

1 cup canola oil plus 2 tablespoons for sautéing

2 tablespoons sesame seeds (toasted to light brown)

3 cloves garlic (chopped small, chunky)

4 cups cauliflower florets (cooked, chopped small)

Salt and pepper to taste

1 tablespoon toasted sesame seeds plus 1 tablespoon for garnish

½ cup white balsamic vinegar

1 head romaine lettuce

2 cups cherry tomatoes

1. Heat a medium-sized sauté pan to medium heat. Add 2 tablespoons of canola oil to the pan and heat for 20 seconds, then add the sesame seeds and garlic.

2. Stir the mixture to prevent the garlic from burning and, after 1 minute, add the cauliflower, salt, and pepper. Sauté for 1 minute and set aside.

3. In a small mixing bowl, add the remaining 1 cup canola oil, 1 tablespoon sesame oil, vinegar, salt, and pepper and whisk rapidly to combine.

4. In a large salad bowl, add the lettuce and tomatoes. Coat the salad with the dressing and toss well with 2 large wooden spoons.

5. Divide the salad evenly onto 4 plates, top with a generous amount of the cauliflower mixture, garnish with sesame seeds, and serve.

GET THE **EDGE**

This naturally gluten-free salad is so easy to make and adds variety and fabulous taste to any meal. Most people are presented with cauliflower in the form of a full floret. In this recipe the cauliflower is chopped up into bite-size pieces, which makes it easier to eat as well as easier to combine with the other ingredients.

WILD MUSHROOM AND ROSEMARY POLENTA SALAD

SERVES 4 | Calories: 693 | Protein: 19 grams | Carbohydrates: 51 grams | Fiber: 5 grams | Fat: 47 grams | Sodium: 774 milligrams

6 tablespoons olive oil

4 tablespoons soy butter

1 tablespoon rosemary (fresh, chopped fine)

1 shallot (minced)

Salt and pepper to taste

1½ cups GF Homemade Chicken Stock (see recipe in Sauces, Stocks, and Special Additions)

1 cup soy cream

1 cup soy milk

1 cup cornmeal

2 cups assorted wild mushrooms (rough chopped)

8 cups assorted salad greens

2 Roma tomatoes (small dice)

1 cup shaved Parmigiano-Reggiano

1. Heat a medium-sized soup pot to medium heat, then add 2 tablespoons of oil and all the butter.

2. Add the rosemary, shallot, salt, and pepper and stir with wooden spoon to combine. After 1 minute, add the stock, cream, and milk, stir well, and bring to a boil.

3. Remove from the heat and, while whisking the mixture, sprinkle in the cornmeal.

4. Place pot on low heat and continue whisking until the polenta thickens. Once thick, pour into a greased baking pan and set aside.

5. Meanwhile, heat a medium-sized sauté pan to medium-high heat for 20 seconds, then add 3 tablespoons of oil. Wait 10 seconds and add the mushrooms.

6. Sauté the mushrooms for 3 minutes then add them into the polenta.

7. Cover 4 dinner plates with the salad greens and sprinkle the tomatoes and 1 tablespoon of oil over the greens on each plate.

8. Cut the polenta into 8 pieces. Put 2 pieces over each other on each of the dinner plates, garnish with cheese shavings, and serve.

GET THE **EDGE**

There might be days that you will crave a carbohydrate to fill you up in place of gluten-containing grains. The polenta—which is made from gluten-free corn—in this salad is a perfect choice to fill this need.

SIDES

These delicious, gluten-free side dishes complement the Entrées in the next section by providing additional vitamins, minerals, and fiber to form a balanced meal. These side dishes incorporate a wide variety of vegetables and beans that are seasoned with fresh herbs and spices for natural added flavor. Enjoy!

SIDES CONTENTS

SNOW PEAS WITH WATER CHESTNUTS AND GINGER

SERVES 4 | Calories: 397 | Protein: 7 grams | Carbohydrates: 14 grams | Fiber: 4 grams | Fat: 36 grams | Sodium: 518 milligrams

1 pound snow pea pods, ends trimmed

½ cup peanut oil

1 8-ounce can water chestnuts, drained, rinsed, and sliced

½ cup unsalted peanuts

2 tablespoons soy sauce

1 teaspoon lemon juice

1 tablespoon minced fresh gingerroot

Tabasco or other red pepper sauce to taste

1. Place the snow pea pods in a hot wok or frying pan with the oil. Stir to coat, then add the water chestnuts and peanuts, stirring again.

2. Continue cooking, and after 5 minutes, add the rest of the ingredients. Mix well and serve hot or at room temperature.

PUMPKIN RISOTTO

SERVES 4 | Calories: 345 | Protein: 15 grams | Carbohydrates: 29 grams | Fiber: 2 grams | Fat: 20 grams | Sodium: 1046 milligrams

2 cups fresh pumpkin, peeled, seeded, and cut into dice

Water to cover the pumpkin

1 tablespoon salt

5 cups GF Homemade Chicken Stock (see recipe in Sauces, Stocks, and Special Additions)

4 tablespoons butter

½ cup finely chopped sweet onion

2 teaspoons dried sage or 1 tablespoon chopped fresh

½ teaspoon dried oregano or 2 teaspoons chopped fresh

1½ cups arborio rice

Salt and pepper to taste

½ cup Parmesan cheese

¼ cup pepitas, for garnish

1. Put the diced pumpkin in a saucepan with water to cover and lightly salt. Simmer until the pumpkin is just tender, drain, and with a hand blender, proceed to puree the pumpkin in a small mixing bowl, reserving liquid, and set aside.

2. Heat the chicken stock in a large saucepan and keep at a low simmer.

3. Melt the butter in a big, heavy pot and add onion; sauté until soft. Add the sage, oregano, rice, salt, and pepper.

4. Slowly add the stock to the rice, ¼ cup at a time. When the pot hisses, add more stock, ¼ cup at a time. Repeat until stock is gone and then, if rice is still dry, add some of the pumpkin liquid.

5. Stir in the pumpkin and Parmesan cheese. Add extra pepper or butter if desired. Garnish with a sprinkle of pepitas and serve immediately.

GET THE **EDGE**

When you can get fresh pumpkin, peeled, seeded, and chopped, at the grocery store, go for it! Otherwise, it's easy to cut a pumpkin in half, remove the seeds, and place it cut-side down in a baking dish. Add ½ inch of water, cover with foil, and roast it for an hour or more in a 250°F oven. Then it's easy to purée. That is an excellent way to prepare pumpkin for pies and soups.

CLASSIC ITALIAN RISOTTO

SERVES 4 | Calories: 314 | Protein: 14 grams | Carbohydrates: 23 grams | Fiber: 1 gram | Fat: 19 grams | Sodium: 930 milligrams

5 cups GF Homemade Chicken Stock or GF Homemade Vegetable Stock (see recipes in Sauces, Stocks, and Special Additions)

2 tablespoons butter

2 tablespoons olive oil

½ cup finely chopped sweet onion

2 stalks celery, finely chopped

¼ cup celery leaves, chopped

1½ cups arborio rice

1 teaspoon salt, or to taste

⅔ cup freshly grated Parmesan cheese

¼ cup chopped parsley

Freshly ground black pepper to taste

1. Bring the stock to a slow simmer over low heat and keep it hot.

2. Place the butter and oil in a heavy-bottomed pot, melt butter, and add the onion, celery, and celery leaves. Cook for 8–10 minutes.

3. Add the rice and stir to coat with butter and oil. Stir in salt.

4. In ¼-cup increments, start adding hot stock. Stir until the stock has been absorbed into the rice. Add another ¼ cup, stirring until all of the stock is absorbed. Repeat this process until all of the hot stock is gone. It must be stirred constantly and takes about 35 minutes. (A stirring helper is nice.)

5. When all of the stock is gone, taste the rice. If it needs more stock or water, add it and keep stirring. Add the cheese, parsley, and pepper. Serve immediately.

GET THE EDGE

Risotto should be very creamy on the outside, with just a bit of toothsome resistance on the inside of each grain of rice.

MEDITERRANEAN RICE WITH SAFFRON AND CHERRIES

SERVES 6 TO 8 | Calories: 234 | Protein: 7 grams | Carbohydrates: 28 grams | Fiber: 2 grams | Fat: 11 grams | Sodium: 418 milligrams

1 tablespoon butter or olive oil

1½ cups basmati or other short-grain rice

2½ cups GF Homemade Chicken Stock (see recipe in Sauces, Stocks, and Special Additions)

1 teaspoon saffron threads

1 cup fresh cherries with juice (pitted and stemmed)

1 tablespoon butter

1 teaspoon salt

Freshly ground pepper to taste

½ cup slivered almonds, toasted, for garnish

1. Heat the butter or oil and add the rice; cook, stirring, for 6 minutes.

2. Add the chicken stock and bring to a boil. Reduce heat to low and add all but the nuts.

3. Cover and simmer for 25 minutes, or until the rice is tender. Check the rice every 10 minutes to make sure it does not dry out. If the rice is stubbornly tough, add more stock, or water.

4. Place in a warm serving bowl and sprinkle with almonds.

GET THE **EDGE**

You can also use a 15-ounce can unsweetened sour cherries or 1 pound sour red pie cherries, but do not use sweetened pie cherries in this recipe due to their high gluten content. Interestingly, you can also use summer fruit, tropical fruit, dried fruit, and just about any kind of nut with white rice or wild rice.

EGGPLANT ROMANO STACK

SERVES 4 | Calories: 436 | Protein: 21 grams | Carbohydrates: 38 grams | Fiber: 10 grams | Fat: 23 grams | Sodium: 373 milligrams

1 large eggplant (peeled and sliced into ¼" disks)

Salt

½ cup olive oil

2 cups garbanzo/fava bean flour

2 eggs

2 tablespoons water

Canola oil spray

1 cup Parmesan cheese (grated fine, reserve ¼ cup for garnish)

2 large tomatoes (sliced thin)

1 cup fresh basil

Salt and black pepper to taste

1 medium yellow onion (sliced thin)

1 tablespoon dried oregano

1. Preheat oven to 375°F and spray an 8" x 8" Pyrex dish or 8–10" round soufflé dish with oil.

2. Lay out eggplant disks on paper towels and sprinkle with a pinch of salt, to draw out the moisture. Let sit for 20 minutes.

3. Meanwhile, heat a large sauté pan to medium-high heat and add the oil.

4. Pour the flour onto a large plate. Then crack the eggs into a medium-size mixing bowl, add the water, and blend well.

5. Take an eggplant disk and dust it in the flour, then cover it in the egg, then cover it with the flour.

6. Sauté the eggplant for about 2–3 minutes or until golden brown. Remove to a plate covered in a paper towel to drain the oil. Continue this process with all the eggplant disks.

7. Place a layer of the cooked eggplant disks on the bottom of your soufflé dish. Sprinkle with some of the cheese. Add a layer of tomatoes and sprinkle with basil, salt, and pepper to taste. Then, add a layer of onions and sprinkle with oregano. Repeat until all the eggplant is used and is the very top layer.

8. Sprinkle the remainder of the cheese on top and place in the oven for 25 minutes. Cut with a sharp knife into wedges and serve.

Blueberry Pancakes

Tomato Basil Soup

Grilled Shrimp Salad

Pomegranate Chicken

White Clam Pizza

Zucchini Boats with King Crab

Lentils and Cabbage

Panna Cotta

SWEET POTATOES WITH LEEKS AND ONIONS

SERVES 4 TO 6 | Calories: 683 | Protein: 8 grams | Carbohydrates: 61 grams | Fiber: 8 grams | Fat: 47 grams | Sodium: 813 milligrams

2 leeks, white part only, rinsed and chopped

2 large sweet onions such as Vidalias

2 stalks celery with tops, finely chopped

4 tablespoons olive oil or butter

4 sweet potatoes, peeled and sliced thinly

1 teaspoon dried thyme

Salt and pepper to taste

Soy milk to cover (other milks are all fine if soy is a problem)

1½ cups gluten-free corn bread crumbs

Butter or margarine for topping

1. Preheat the oven to 325°F.

2. Sauté the leeks, onions, and celery in olive oil or butter, and then prepare an oval metal or pottery gratin pan with nonstick spray.

3. Layer the sweet potato slices in the gratin pan with the vegetables. Sprinkle with thyme, salt, and pepper as you go along.

4. Finish with a layer of potatoes. Add the milk until it meets the top layer of potatoes. Then add the corn bread crumbs. Dot with extra butter or margarine.

5. Bake until the potatoes are soft, about 1 hour. Add more milk if dish starts to dry out.

CAULIFLOWER "MASHED POTATOES"

SERVES 4 | Calories: 151 | Protein: 7 grams | Carbohydrates: 13 grams | Fiber: 5 grams | Fat: 8 grams | Sodium: 271 milligrams

1 head of fresh cauliflower (separated into florets)

2 tablespoons unsalted butter or soy butter

Salt and pepper to taste

2 cups plain soy milk

1 teaspoon wasabi paste

1. In a medium to large microwave-safe bowl, add cauliflower and butter. Microwave on high for 4 minutes or until tender.

2. Transfer the cauliflower to your food processor; add salt and pepper. Pulse to break up the florets to pea-size pieces.

3. Through the top feeder of the processor, stream in the soy milk to desired consistency. With processor still running, add the wasabi paste and run until fully incorporated. Taste the mixture, adjust flavors, and serve.

RATATOUILLE

SERVES 4 | Calories: 207 | Protein: 3 grams | Carbohydrates: 20 grams | Fiber: 5 grams | Fat: 14 grams | Sodium: 17 milligrams

4 tablespoons olive oil

2 cups red onion (medium chopped)

2 medium zucchini or yellow squash (cut into ½" cubes)

½ eggplant (peeled, cut into ½" cubes)

2 cups roasted red pepper (cut into ½" squares)

2 garlic cloves (minced)

2 cups tomatoes (medium chopped)

2 tablespoons dried oregano

2 tablespoons fresh basil (chopped fine)

Salt and pepper to taste

1. Heat a large sauté pan to medium-high heat. Add oil to pan and heat for 30 seconds, then add onion and sauté for 2 minutes.

2. Add zucchini, eggplant, red pepper, garlic, and tomatoes. Stir and sauté for 3 minutes, then add the oregano, basil, salt, and pepper and blend them into the mixture. Continue to sauté the mixture for 3 more minutes, remove from heat, and serve.

ROASTED GARLIC ARTICHOKE

SERVES 4 | Calories: 354 | Protein: 7 grams | Carbohydrates: 26 grams | Fiber: 12 grams | Fat: 26 grams | Sodium: 248 milligrams

1 head of garlic (top cut off and brushed with olive oil)

4 medium or large fresh artichokes (halved)

4 tablespoons unsalted butter or soy butter

1 medium red onion (peeled and quartered)

2 medium to large tomatoes (quartered)

Salt and pepper to taste

4 tablespoons olive oil

4 tablespoons Parmesan cheese (grated fine)

1. Preheat oven to 400°F. Enclose garlic in foil "pouch" and bake for 45 minutes, then set aside to cool. When cool, squeeze the roasted garlic out into a small bowl and set aside. Keep oven on.

2. Combine artichokes and butter and microwave on high for 2 minutes.

3. Transfer artichokes to baking dish with onions and tomatoes, sprinkle with salt and pepper, then spread roasted garlic on the cut side of the artichoke halves. Spoon the oil over the onion and tomatoes.

4. Bake for 8–10 minutes, then transfer vegetables to a serving plate, sprinkle with the grated cheese, and serve.

GET THE **EDGE**

Artichokes are available all year and are at their peak from March through May. They contain vitamin C and niacin and a small amount of protein and are loaded with fiber and low in fat, which makes them perfect for weight loss.

EGGPLANT STACK WITH AVOCADO, HUMMUS, AND ROASTED PEPPER

SERVES 4 | Calories: 309 | Protein: 6 grams | Carbohydrates: 18 grams | Fiber: 8 grams | Fat: 25 grams | Sodium: 382 milligrams

1 fresh eggplant (peeled and cut into 24 ¼" disks)

Salt

4 tablespoons canola oil

1 cup hummus

1 ripe avocado (halved, pitted, and cut into ¼" slices)

1 cup roasted red peppers (julienned)

4 tablespoons fresh basil (stemmed and cut into fine slivers)

Salt and pepper to taste

1. Lay 24 eggplant disks on paper towels and sprinkle with salt, to draw out the moisture, for 20 minutes.

2. Heat a medium-size sauté pan to medium-high heat. Add the oil and heat for 30 seconds, then add the eggplant. Sauté eggplant for approximately 2 minutes or until lightly browned on both sides, then remove to a plate covered with a paper towel to drain the excess oil.

3. Place 2 eggplant disks, on top of each other but slightly askew, on a serving plate and top with a generous layer of hummus. Add 2 more slices of eggplant, slightly askew, and top with 2 slices of avocado. Top with 2 more eggplant disks, slightly askew, then top with red peppers. Repeat the process until you have 4 plates assembled. Sprinkle with basil, salt, and pepper and serve.

ZUCCHINI, TOMATO, AND PORTOBELLO ROULADE

SERVES 4 | Calories: 536 | Protein: 10 grams | Carbohydrates: 7 grams | Fiber: 2 grams | Fat: 30 grams | Sodium: 333 milligrams

4 tablespoons olive oil

2 large portobello mushrooms (stem removed, cut into ¼" slices)

2 Roma tomatoes (cut into small dice)

4 tablespoons fresh basil (stemmed, sliced into fine slivers)

Salt and pepper to taste

2 large zucchinis (mandoline-sliced into ribbons)

1 cup goat cheese

1. Heat a large sauté pan to medium heat. Add oil and heat for 30 seconds, then add the mushroom slices and sauté for 2 minutes. Add tomatoes, half the basil, salt, and pepper. Sauté for 1 minute and then set aside to cool.

2. Place 4 of the zucchini ribbons in the sauté pan (being careful not to overlap) and sauté for 30 seconds on each side. Then remove to a serving plate, overlapping the side edges by ¼" on a large piece of plastic wrap, and let cool.

3. Spoon ¼ of the mushroom mixture on top of the ribbons, leaving 1" of zucchini showing on all sides.

4. Add ¼ of the goat cheese evenly across the lower part of the ribbons, leaving 1" of zucchini showing on both sides.

5. Grab the end of the plastic wrap and fold the lower part over the cheese. Continue to roll the zucchini until the roll is complete. With the roll still in the plastic wrap, transfer it to a serving plate and then unwrap. Repeat the assembly process to make 4 rolls, sprinkle with the remaining basil, and serve.

GET THE **EDGE**

The fresh basil and pepper help to enhance the natural flavor of the vegetables in this dish. Make sure your spice rack is always stocked with fresh gluten-free herbs and spices so you can add flavor to your favorite foods without adding fat and calories.

BRUSSELS SPROUTS WITH CHICKEN

SERVES 4 | Calories: 209 | Protein: 12 grams | Carbohydrates: 11 grams | Fiber: 4 grams | Fat: 14 grams | Sodium: 198 milligrams

4 tablespoons extra-virgin olive oil

1 cup yellow onion (fine chopped)

1 pound fresh Brussels sprouts (halved)

1 cup chicken (chopped fine)

2 garlic cloves (fine chopped)

1 tablespoon fresh thyme

Salt and pepper to taste

1. Heat a medium sauté pan to medium-high heat. Add olive oil and heat for 30 seconds, then add the onion and Brussels sprouts. Sauté until the onions become opaque, roughly 2 minutes.

2. Add the chicken, garlic, thyme, salt, and pepper to the pan and gently combine. Turn heat to low, cover for 3 minutes, and serve.

GET THE **EDGE**

Like most vegetables, Brussels sprouts are low in fat and calories. What makes them unique as a vegetable is that they are also high in protein; in fact, protein makes up more than a quarter of their calories. Protein is the building block of muscle in the body and will help normalize your blood sugar levels to reduce the craving for sweet food.

BAKED BBQ BEANS

SERVES 4 | Calories: 230 | Protein: 9 grams | Carbohydrates: 38 grams | Fiber: 9 grams | Fat: 5 grams | Sodium: 1071 milligrams

2 tablespoons canola oil

1 cup white onion (chopped small)

2 garlic cloves (minced fine)

2 tablespoons raw brown sugar

2 cups Sidney's GF BBQ Sauce (see recipe in Sauces, Stocks, and Special Additions)

Salt and black pepper to taste

3 15-ounce cans kidney beans (rinsed and well drained)

1. Heat a medium-size saucepan to medium heat. Add the oil and heat for 20 seconds, then add the onion and garlic. Cook for 1 minute and add the sugar to the pan.

2. Add the BBQ sauce and stir. Taste the mixture, add salt and pepper, and continue to stir the sauce until combined well.

3. Add the beans and stir gently for 20 seconds. Reduce the heat to low and cook for 3 minutes until the beans are hot. Serve.

GET THE EDGE

This recipe is tastier than ordinary baked beans because of the added gluten-free barbecue sauce and other zesty ingredients. Most canned baked beans contain molasses and preservatives for shelf life, but we've eliminated all of these unhealthy ingredients for a more natural, fresh flavor. If you don't want to make your own gluten-free barbecue sauce, you can find it at most health-food supermarkets.

BROCCOLI PARMESANO

SERVES 4 | Calories: 241 | Protein: 12 grams | Carbohydrates: 6 grams | Fiber: <1 gram | Fat: 20 grams | Sodium: 548 milligrams

3 tablespoons olive oil

1 tablespoon unsalted butter

3 garlic cloves (sliced thin)

1 tablespoon lemon zest

1 tablespoon lemon juice

Salt and pepper

4 cups broccoli florets (rinsed)

1 cup Parmigiano-Reggiano cheese (shaved)

1. Heat a large sauté pan to medium heat. Add oil and heat for 20 seconds then add the butter. Heat for 20 seconds then add the garlic, lemon zest, juice, salt, and pepper and stir to combine.

2. Add the broccoli and, with a large spoon, fold the broccoli over continuously for 30 seconds to coat well and top with the shaved cheese.

3. Turn the heat to low, cover the pan, and cook for 3 minutes more.

4. Transfer the broccoli into a medium-sized serving bowl and serve.

CABBAGE AND RED ONIONS

SERVES 4 | Calories: 197 | Protein: 5 grams | Carbohydrates: 24 grams | Fiber: 8 grams | Fat: 10 grams | Sodium: 353 milligrams

3 tablespoons canola oil

1 red onion (halved, sliced thin)

1 green cabbage (shredded medium)

1 tablespoon celery salt

Black pepper to taste

1. Heat a large sauté pan to medium-high heat. Add the oil and heat for 20 seconds, then add the sliced onion to the pan. Sauté the onion for 2 minutes to soften and allow sweetness to emerge.

2. Add the cabbage on top of the onion (do not stir to combine) and then season with celery salt and pepper. Let cook for 30 seconds, then fold the onions from underneath the cabbage to the top with cooking tongs.

3. Continue to toss the cabbage every 30 seconds until it cooks to desired crispness or softness. Remove to a serving bowl and serve.

GET THE EDGE

Celery salt, which gives the dish a little extra tang, is one of the unique ingredients in this recipe. This type of salt is made with the dried seeds of the celery plant and is useful in providing a celery taste to foods when actual celery is not used in the recipe. Celery salt is available in the spice section at many markets.

CARROT CHIPS

SERVES 4 | Calories: 283 | Protein: <1 gram | Carbohydrates: 6 grams | Fiber: 1 gram | Fat: 28 grams | Sodium: 182 milligrams

2 tablespoons white balsamic vinegar

1 cup canola oil

1 tablespoon lemon juice

1 teaspoon raw sugar

1 tablespoon oregano

Salt and pepper to taste

3 large carrots (peeled, cut into ¼ slices on the bias)

1. In a small mixing bowl add all the ingredients except the carrots. Whisk together for 30 seconds or until well combined.

2. Add the carrots, and stir them with the dressing for 30 seconds until coated. Let the carrots marinate in the dressing for 30 minutes, remove them to a serving bowl, and serve.

GET THE **EDGE**

Carrots are "slow-releasers" of sugar, which means that they release naturally occurring sugar into your bloodstream. This will give you an energy boost over an extended period of time. Carrot chips make a perfect snack for the kids to replace fried, store-bought chips; they are also great to serve with one of the lettuce wrap recipes in the Entrées section of this book.

DAIRY-FREE CELERY SALT COLESLAW

SERVES 4 | Calories: 517 | Protein: 1 gram | Carbohydrates: 2 grams | Fiber: <1 gram | Fat: 57 grams | Sodium: 647 milligrams

1 egg yolk

1 teaspoon mustard (dry)

1 tablespoon rice wine vinegar

1 teaspoon raw sugar

1 teaspoon celery salt

1 tablespoon cracked black pepper (for a spicy kick, also add a teaspoon of cayenne pepper)

1 tablespoon lime juice

1 cup canola oil

1 14-ounce bag raw coleslaw mix (not dressed)

1 cup fresh cilantro (rough chopped)

1. In a medium-sized mixing bowl add the egg yolk, mustard, vinegar, sugar, celery salt, and pepper and whisk rapidly to combine for 30 seconds.

2. Add ½ of the lime juice and stream in half of the oil while whisking vigorously to emulsify the mixture.

3. Proceed to add the rest of the juice and then immediately stream in the rest of the oil. The result will be a celery salt mayonnaise.

4. In a serving bowl, combine the mayonnaise with the cilantro and coleslaw mix, and serve.

HARVEST MOON BUTTERNUT SQUASH

SERVES 4 | Calories: 126 | Protein: 1 gram | Carbohydrates: 20 grams | Fiber: <1 gram | Fat: 6 grams | Sodium: 297 milligrams

1 large butternut squash (halved, cleaned)

2 tablespoons honey

1 tablespoon cinnamon

1 teaspoon fresh ground nutmeg

Salt and pepper to taste

2 tablespoons unsalted butter

1. Place both halves of the squash cut side up on a microwavable plate. Cover cut side of squash with the honey, using a rubber spatula or butter knife.

2. Sprinkle squash with cinnamon, nutmeg, salt, and pepper. Place half of the butter in the cavity of each squash half and wrap the squash in plastic wrap.

3. Microwave squash for 7 minutes. Let cool for 2 minutes then carefully trim all the skin off with a sharp kitchen knife.

4. Cut squash into 1" cubes, place in a serving bowl, and serve.

GET THE **EDGE**

Butternut squash is inherently a sweet and satisfying vegetable and makes a perfect side dish. Squash is high in fiber and is very filling, which makes it an excellent choice for weight control. Butternut squash is loaded with vitamin A and is also fat-, cholesterol-, and sodium-free. Try butternut squash with any of the seafood recipes in the Entrées section of this book.

ROASTED CORN WITH RED PEPPER AND ONION

SERVES 4 | Calories: 239 | Protein: 3 grams | Carbohydrates: 23 grams | Fiber: 3 grams | Fat: 17 grams | Sodium: 230 milligrams

3 tablespoons soy butter

3 ears of fresh corn (shucked and trimmed)

1 cup fresh cilantro (chopped medium)

2 tablespoons canola oil

1 large red pepper (cleaned, cut into ½" dice)

1 yellow onion (chopped small)

1 tablespoon cumin (ground)

Salt and pepper to taste

1. Spread 1 tablespoon of butter on each ear of corn, wrap corn in plastic wrap, and microwave for 3 minutes on high.

2. Remove corn to a plate and let cool for 5 minutes before carefully removing the kernels with a sharp knife. Set aside.

3. Heat a medium sauté pan to medium-high heat. Add the oil to the pan and heat for 20 seconds, then add the red pepper, onions, cumin, salt, and pepper.

4. Sauté for 2 minutes, then add the corn and cilantro to the pan. Sauté the mixture for 1 minute or to your desired doneness, remove to a serving bowl, and serve.

SPINACH WITH MUSHROOMS, SHALLOTS, AND RED ONION

SERVES 4 | Calories: 283 | Protein: 12 grams | Carbohydrates: 21 grams | Fiber: 6 grams | Fat: 20 grams | Sodium: 436 milligrams

2 tablespoons canola oil

4 tablespoons unsalted butter

2 cups white button mushrooms (cleaned, chopped small)

1 cup red onion (chopped small)

2 shallots (chopped fine)

2 24-ounce bags of fresh spinach (rinsed dry, stems removed, cut small with scissors)

Salt and pepper to taste

1. Heat a large sauté pan to medium-high heat. Add the oil and heat for 20 seconds, then add the butter, mushrooms, onion, and shallots. Stir to combine for 1 minute.

2. Continue to sauté for another minute before adding the spinach leaves, salt, and pepper. Sauté the spinach mixture for 3 more minutes or until completely cooked through.

3. Remove the spinach mixture to a serving bowl, and serve.

TUSCAN GREEN BEANS

SERVES 4 | Calories: 158 | Protein: 3 grams | Carbohydrates: 16 grams | Fiber: 5 grams | Fat: 10 grams | Sodium: 160 milligrams

3 tablespoons olive oil

1 cup red onion (sliced thin)

2 cloves garlic (minced fine)

2 tablespoons oregano (dried)

Salt and pepper to taste

1 Roma tomato (cut into small dice)

4 cups fresh green beans (trimmed, washed, and rinsed dry)

1. Heat a large sauté pan to medium heat. Add the oil and heat for 30 seconds, then add the onion, garlic, oregano, salt, pepper, and tomato. Cook for 1 minute so the mixture can begin to release all its flavors, then add the beans and stir to combine. Continue cooking for 3 more minutes.

2. Transfer the beans to a serving bowl and serve.

AMANDA'S CORN CAKE AND CRANBERRIES

SERVES 4 | Calories: 384 | Protein: 2 grams | Carbohydrates: 58 grams | Fiber: 2 grams | Fat: 17 grams | Sodium: 156 milligrams

½ cup unsalted butter (melted)

¼ teaspoon salt

1 teaspoon cayenne pepper (optional)

¾ cup cornmeal

¾ cup raw brown sugar

2 tablespoons soy cream

½ teaspoon baking powder

1 cup dried cranberries

1 cup fresh corn (cut off the cob)

1. Preheat oven to 350°F.

2. Add the melted butter, salt, cayenne pepper (if a little heat is desired), and cornmeal to a food processor bowl and pulse 10 times. Then add the sugar, cream, and baking powder to the bowl and let run for 30 seconds. Then add the cranberries and corn and pulse for just 4 times.

3. Spoon a generous dollop of the corn cake mixture into each of eight cups of a nonstick cupcake pan. Bake for 50 minutes or until the cakes are golden brown and a toothpick comes out dry. Remove to small baking rack to cool, or serve immediately with your favorite dish.

INDIAN CORN CAKES

MAKES ABOUT 12 CAKES | Calories: 324 | Protein: 4 grams | Carbohydrates: 58 grams | Fiber: 3 grams | Fat: 8 grams | Sodium: 512 milligrams

7 cups water

1 tablespoon salt, or to taste

2 cups cornmeal

½ teaspoon freshly ground black pepper, or to taste

1 teaspoon molasses

1 cup red currants

4 tablespoons butter

1. Prepare an 11" x 13" Pyrex lasagna pan with nonstick spray.

2. Bring the water to a boil and add the salt. Stir in the cornmeal and cook for about 20 minutes, stirring. Add the pepper, molasses, and red currants.

3. Spread the corn mixture in the lasagna pan and cover. Refrigerate for 1–2 hours or until very stiff.

4. Heat the butter in a large sauté pan. Cut the corn cakes into squares and fry until golden on both sides.

ENTRÉES

This section includes a selection of world-class, gourmet entrées that are perfect to serve for both lunch and dinner. We recommend choosing organic poultry and vegetables and wild, fresh seafood for flavor and quality.

ENTRÉES CONTENTS

ROASTED GARLIC CHICKEN BREAST PROVENÇAL

SERVES 4 | Calories: 494 | Protein: 54 grams | Carbohydrates: 16 grams | Fiber: 3 grams | Fat: 24 grams | Sodium: 458 milligrams

2 garlic heads

5 tablespoons olive oil

2 cups yellow onion (thin sliced)

4 8-ounce boneless, skinless chicken breasts

3 tablespoons fresh rosemary (fine chopped)

1 cup black or green olives (sliced)

1 cup Roma tomatoes

Salt and cracked black pepper to taste

4 rosemary sprigs (for garnish)

1. Preheat oven to 425°F.

2. With a sharp knife, cut off the top of the garlic and discard. Place the garlic on a piece of tin foil, add 1 tablespoon of oil, and sprinkle with a pinch of salt. Gather the foil into a pouch to enclose the garlic heads and place in the oven for 45 minutes.

3. Remove pouch from the oven, open, and let cool for 5 minutes. Then, remove the garlic heads and squeeze until all the garlic oozes out onto a small dish.

4. Meanwhile, bring a medium-sized sauté pan to medium temperature. Add the remaining oil and heat for 30 seconds. Add the onions and cook until opaque. Add the chicken, rosemary, olives, tomatoes, salt, and pepper.

5. Cover the pan and cook for 10 minutes. Remove just the chicken breasts and spread roasted garlic on each one, covering the entire top of the chicken. Pour the remaining contents of the sauté pan on a serving plate, place the chicken breasts on top, garnish with a rosemary sprig, and serve.

GET THE EDGE

Garlic reduces cholesterol and triglycerides, prevents cancer, and fights infections—and, according to scientists at the Weizmann Institute of Science, helps with weight loss.

POBLANO CHICKEN

SERVES 4 | Calories: 601 | Protein: 69 grams | Carbohydrates: 34 grams | Fiber: 4 grams |
Fat: 17 grams | Sodium: 318 milligrams

4 poblano chili peppers

4 garlic cloves (minced fine)

1 cup Spanish onion (chopped medium)

1 cup cilantro (rough chopped; reserve a pinch for presentation)

4 teaspoons lime juice

4 8-ounce boneless chicken breasts (salt and peppered, seared in canola oil, and cut into 1" cubes)

Salt and pepper to taste

3 teaspoons canola oil

2 cups shredded mozzarella cheese

1 cup cornmeal

1. Preheat oven to 400°F

2. With a sharp paring knife, trace the top of each poblano chili and remove it to make a cavity for the chicken filling.

3. Fine-chop the removed top of the chili and add to a medium-sized mixing bowl.

4. Add the garlic, onion, cilantro, lime juice, and chicken to the bowl and blend together. Add salt and pepper and set aside.

5. Line a baking sheet with tin foil. Brush the chilies all over with oil and place on baking sheet.

6. Fill each chili with the mixture generously. Cover the filling with mozzarella and sprinkle with cornmeal. Bake the chilies for 20–25 minutes. Sprinkle a pinch of cilantro over the filling and serve.

GET THE **EDGE**

Cooking healthy meals at home will help to reduce the temptation to eat fast food that is high in fat and oversized. The intense but mild flavor of the poblano pepper is a great complement to the succulent chicken. This is a gourmet Mexican dish. The tapioca or soy cheese makes this recipe safe for those who are lactose intolerant. Both of these cheeses taste great! The soy cheese has more nutritional value but the tapioca cheese is a good choice for those who cannot tolerate soy.

POMEGRANATE CHICKEN

SERVES 4 | Calories: 750 | Protein: 54 grams | Carbohydrates: 89 grams | Fiber: 4 grams | Fat: 24 grams | Sodium: 132 milligrams

12 ounces clear rice noodles

6 tablespoons canola oil

Salt and pepper to taste

4 8-ounce boneless, skinless chicken breast

8 green onions (cut into ¼" diagonal slices)

4 garlic cloves (fine chopped)

1 navel orange (skin julienned and reserved, juice reserved)

2 cups pomegranate seeds (reserve ¼ cup to garnish)

GET THE **EDGE**

All the ingredients in this recipe are naturally gluten-free! As a bonus, this recipe is packed with antioxidants, which provide your body with the nutritional support it needs to keep strong and full of energy during the weight-loss process.

1. Soak rice noodles in warm water for 5 minutes or until soft. Drain noodles well.

2. Heat a medium sauté pan to medium-high heat and add canola oil, wait 30 seconds, then add rice noodles to pan and flatten with a spatula into a pancake. Sauté until light brown on both sides and remove to a plate lined with paper towels to drain oil.

3. Sprinkle salt and pepper on chicken breast and add to already heated sauté pan. Sear for 1 minute per side.

4. Turn heat down to medium low and add green onions, garlic, ¼ cup julienned orange skin, orange juice, and ¼ cup of pomegranate seeds and cover. Cook for 7 minutes or to desired doneness.

5. Place rice noodle pancake on serving plate. Pour contents of sauté pan on top, sprinkle with remaining pomegranate seeds. Repeat until all pancakes are made, then serve.

CHINESE SIZZLING RICE WITH CHICKEN

SERVES 4 | Calories: 516 | Protein: 16 grams | Carbohydrates: 49 grams | Fiber: 7 grams | Fat: 30 grams | Sodium: 1036 milligrams

1 cup canola oil plus 1 tablespoon

4 green onions (fine chopped)

2 tablespoons fresh gingerroot (minced)

Black pepper to taste

3 garlic cloves (minced)

4 6-ounce boneless, skinless chicken thighs (cooked, cut into 1" dice)

2 cups Chinese snow peas

1 cup bamboo shoots

1 cup water chestnuts (sliced)

1 cup baby ears of corn

3 cups bean sprouts

4 tablespoons tamari sauce

1 cup cilantro (fine chopped)

2 cups long grain white or brown rice (cooked)

1. In a medium-sized sauté pan add 1 tablespoon of oil. Bring the pan to medium heat and add the green onions, gingerroot, pepper, and garlic. Sauté for 30 seconds, then mix in the chicken, snow peas, bamboo shoots, water chestnuts, corn, and sprouts.

2. After 1 minute add in the tamari and cilantro until heated through. Turn heat to low.

3. Heat a medium-sized sauté pan to medium-high heat. Add the remaining 1 cup oil and heat until it starts to ripple. Add the cooked rice and flatten into a pancake. Sauté until crispy brown on both sides then remove to serving plate. Top the crispy rice pancake with chicken mixture and serve.

CRISPY CHICKEN WITH HOISIN SAUCE

SERVES 4 | Calories: 718 | Protein: 56 grams | Carbohydrates: 42 grams | Fiber: 4 grams | Fat: 36 grams | Sodium: 1322 milligrams

1 cup cornmeal

Salt and pepper to taste

2 eggs

4 8-ounce boneless, skinless chicken breasts

Canola oil spray

1 cup canola oil

6 green onions (chopped fine)

2 cups Chinese snow peas

2 teaspoon fresh gingerroot

3 garlic cloves (minced)

2 cup bean sprouts

2 cups cilantro

1 cup gluten-free hoisin sauce

1. Preheat oven to 425°F.

2. Prepare a baking sheet with tin foil and set aside. Pour cornmeal on a plate and add salt and pepper.

3. In a small mixing bowl, beat the eggs and a teaspoon of water with a fork and set aside.

4. Coat the chicken with cornmeal and then coat with egg mixture. Coat the chicken again with the cornmeal and place on baking sheet.

5. Spray the chicken breasts lightly with canola spray. Bake 12–15 minutes or until golden brown and remove from oven.

6. Heat a medium-size saucepan to medium-high heat and heat the oil for 30 seconds, then add the green onions, peas, gingerroot, and garlic and sauté for 1 minute.

7. Add the sprouts, cilantro, and hoisin sauce and combine well. Place the chicken on a serving plate, cover with hoisin mixture, and serve.

GET THE **EDGE**

Eating should never be boring when you are trying to lose weight, and using spices is a great way to flavor your food without adding extra fat and calories. You will taste a big difference in the flavor that the whole peppercorns in this recipe provide. One of the best ways to buy black pepper is in whole peppercorn form so you can grind it yourself.

CHOPPED CHICKEN, GINGER, AND TOMATO LETTUCE WRAPS

SERVES 4 | Calories: 376 | Protein: 53 grams | Carbohydrates: 8 grams | Fiber: 2 grams | Fat: 17 grams | Sodium: 641 milligrams

4 tablespoons canola oil

Salt and pepper to taste

4 8-ounce boneless, skinless chicken breasts

3 garlic cloves (minced)

3 teaspoon gingerroot (minced fine)

8 iceberg lettuce leaves

4 green onions (fine chopped)

1½ cups Roma tomato (small dice)

1½ cups radish sprouts

Red pepper flakes to taste

2 tablespoons ginger sauce

1. Heat a medium sauté pan to medium heat. Add oil to pan. Salt and pepper the chicken breasts and then sauté the chicken on both sides for 10 minutes. Add garlic and gingerroot. Continue to cook for 2–3 more minutes or until chicken is cooked through.

2. Remove chicken from pan and let rest for 5 minutes. Cut chicken into small dice and reserve.

3. Open a lettuce leaf and fill with ⅛ of the chicken, green onion, tomato, sprouts, red pepper, and ginger sauce. Repeat the process until all 8 leaves are filled, then serve.

GET THE **EDGE**

Using lettuce as a base is a great way to eat a sandwich without all of that gluten-filled bread. Lettuce is actually a negative calorie food, which means that it actually requires more calories to chew and digest the food than the food contains. This will result in a net loss in calories, which helps burn body fat.

CHICKEN AND CANNELLINI BEANS PROVENÇAL

SERVES 4 | Calories: 444 | Protein: 48 grams | Carbohydrates: 31 grams | Fiber: 7 grams | Fat: 14 grams | Sodium: 526 milligrams

4 tablespoons soy butter

Salt and pepper to taste

3 8-ounce chicken breasts (boneless, skinless, defrosted)

1 medium yellow onion (quartered)

4 cloves garlic (chopped medium)

8 sprigs thyme (fresh, leaves removed) plus 4 for garnish

1 tablespoon cumin (ground)

1 tablespoon rosemary (chopped medium)

2 8-ounce cans cannellini beans (drained well)

2 cups GF Homemade Chicken Stock (see recipe in Sauces, Stocks, and Special Additions)

1. Heat a large sauté pan to medium-high heat and add 2 tablespoons of butter.

2. Salt and pepper the chicken breasts and add to the pan. Sear both sides for 2 minutes each. Turn the heat down to low, remove the chicken, and set aside.

3. Add the onions, garlic, thyme, cumin, and rosemary to the pan and cook for 5 minutes.

4. Cut the chicken into ½" slices and return to the sauté pan. Then add 2 tablespoons of butter, the beans, and stock.

5. Cook for 20–25 minutes, gently stirring every 5 minutes or until the liquid has evaporated. Serve in 4 individual bowls, each garnished with a thyme sprig.

GARLIC SPEAR CHICKEN BREASTS

SERVES 4 | Calories: 413 | Protein: 53 grams | Carbohydrates: 1 gram | Fiber: 0 grams | Fat: 25 grams | Sodium: 197 milligrams

4 8-ounce chicken breasts (boneless, skinless, defrosted)

4 garlic cloves (sliced into ¼" x ½" spears)

Salt and lemon pepper to taste

4 tablespoons canola oil

3 tablespoons soy butter

1 cup parsley (plus ¼ cup for garnish)

1 lemon (sliced into ¼" slices for garnish)

1. On a serving plate, place the chicken breasts with the top, or smooth side, facing up. Then take a chopstick and poke holes ¾ of the way into the chicken about 1" apart. Insert a garlic "spear" into each hole you make then sprinkle the chicken with salt and pepper.

2. Heat a large sauté pan to medium-high heat, add the oil and butter, and heat for 30 seconds. Add the chicken and sauté for 2 minutes on each side to seal in juices.

3. Add the parsley and cover the pan. Turn the heat down to medium low. Cook for 15–18 minutes, until cooked through. Remove from pan to serving dish, garnish with parsley and lemon, and then serve.

LEMON CHICKEN, RICE, AND ARTICHOKE CASSEROLE

SERVES 4 | Calories: 475 | Protein: 35 grams | Carbohydrates: 50 grams | Fiber: 10 grams | Fat: 16 grams | Sodium: 210 milligrams

2 tablespoons canola oil

2 tablespoons soy butter

2 8-ounce chicken breasts (boneless, skinless, defrosted)

1 lemon (½ juiced, ½ sliced into ¼" slices)

Salt and pepper to taste

1 medium yellow onion (chopped medium)

4 cups artichoke hearts (canned or frozen and defrosted)

2 garlic cloves (minced fine)

3 cups brown rice (cooked)

1. Preheat oven to 400°F.

2. Heat a medium sauté pan to medium-high heat and add the oil and butter. Heat for 30 seconds.

3. Sprinkle chicken with lemon juice, salt, and pepper, and add to the pan. Sear both sides for 2 minutes each. Remove chicken and set aside to cool.

4. Reduce heat to medium and add the onions, artichokes, and garlic to the pan. Sauté for 3 minutes and remove to a 13" x 9" Pyrex casserole dish.

5. Add the rice and fold until combined well.

6. Cut the seared chicken in half lengthwise and then slice into ¼" pieces. Add to the casserole dish and combine well.

7. Bake for 20–25 minutes or until the top is golden brown, then let cool for 5 minutes. Garnish each serving with a lemon slice and serve.

SWEET POTATO CRUSTED CHICKEN BREASTS

SERVES 4 | Calories: 454 | Protein: 54 grams | Carbohydrates: 22 grams | Fiber: 3 grams | Fat: 17 grams | Sodium: 281 milligrams

2 sweet potatoes (peeled, cut into 1" pieces)

4 tablespoons soy butter

1 tablespoon cumin (ground)

1 tablespoon brown sugar (raw)

1 tablespoon cinnamon (ground)

Salt and black pepper to taste

Canola spray

4 8-ounce chicken breasts (boneless, skinless, defrosted)

1. Preheat oven to 400°F.

2. Heat a medium-sized saucepan to medium-high heat. Add the potatoes and cover them with water. Add a pinch of salt and bring to a boil. Reduce heat immediately to medium and cook until fork tender, about 25–30 minutes.

3. Drain off all the water from the potatoes and add the butter, cumin, sugar, cinnamon, salt, and pepper. Stir well to combine and then, with a hand blender, purée the mixture and let cool.

4. Line a baking sheet with foil and spray with canola oil.

5. Sprinkle chicken breasts with salt and pepper. With a fork or spoon, coat each breast with the potato purée.

6. Place chicken on baking sheet and bake for 20 minutes or to desired doneness, remove to serving plates, and serve.

GRILLED CHICKEN BREASTS WITH BLUEBERRY SAUCE

SERVES 4 | Calories: 435 | Protein: 54 grams | Carbohydrates: 17 grams | Fiber: 2 grams | Fat: 17 grams | Sodium: 260 milligrams

Canola oil spray

4 8-ounce chicken breasts (boneless, skinless, defrosted)

2 teaspoons cumin (ground)

Salt and pepper to taste

4 tablespoons soy butter

2 garlic cloves (minced)

1 tablespoon raw sugar

2 cups blueberries (fresh, washed)

1. Spray grill or griddle with canola oil, then heat to medium heat.

2. Season the chicken with cumin, salt, and pepper and place on the grill.

3. Grill the chicken for 2 minutes on each side. Then turn over again and rotate to create crossed grill marks. Cook for 5 minutes or until firm to the touch, then remove to serving plate.

4. Heat a small saucepan to medium heat. Add butter, garlic, and sugar. Cook for 1 minute, then add the blueberries to the pan and stir the mixture gently together. Cook for 2 more minutes and remove from heat. Pour the blueberry sauce over the chicken and serve.

STUFFED CHICKEN BREASTS WITH GOAT CHEESE AND BASIL

SERVES 4 | Calories: 529 | Protein: 59 grams | Carbohydrates: 5 grams | Fiber: 1 gram | Fat: 30 grams | Sodium: 426 milligrams

8-ounce chicken breasts (boneless, skinless, defrosted)

8 ounces goat cheese (very cold, cut into 16 ¼" slices)

4 tablespoons basil (fresh leaves, rolled up and sliced into thin ribbons) plus 2 tablespoons for garnish

2 tablespoons garlic powder

Salt and pepper to taste

4 tablespoons olive oil (extra-virgin)

1. Heat a large sauté pan to medium heat.
2. With a sharp knife, cut about a 3"-wide slit into the wider side of each breast. Fill each breast with 2 slices of cheese and 1 tablespoon of basil, then season with garlic powder, salt, and pepper.
3. Add oil to pan and heat for 30 seconds. Add the stuffed chicken to the pan; cover and cook for 10–12 minutes or until firm to the touch.
4. Remove the chicken to a serving dish, sprinkle with reserved basil, and serve.

CHICKEN IN APPLE CIDER AND BRANDY

SERVES 4 TO 6 | Calories: 477 | Protein: 57 grams | Carbohydrates: 8 grams | Fiber: <1 gram | Fat: 19 grams | Sodium: 368 milligrams

2 small chickens, cut into quarters

4 tablespoons butter

1 cup chopped onion

1 tablespoon cornstarch

¼ cup apple brandy or applejack

1¼ cups apple cider

Salt and pepper to taste

½ cup soy cream

1. Rinse and pat the chicken dry. Brown it in butter over medium heat. Add the onion and cook until softened. Stir in the cornstarch.

2. Add the brandy and flame it by setting it on fire with a long match. Be careful not to burn yourself. Add the cider, salt, and pepper. Cover and simmer for 25 minutes.

3. Just before serving, place the chicken on a platter. Add the cream to the sauce in the pan, and heat. Spoon sauce over chicken, sprinkle with your favorite herbs, and serve.

CHICKEN DIVAN

SERVES 6 | Calories: 878 | Protein: 57 grams | Carbohydrates: 24 grams | Fiber: 1 gram | Fat: 62 grams | Sodium: 1013 milligrams

1 pound broccoli florets, cut into bite-size pieces, cooked, and drained

3 pounds chicken breasts, boneless and skinless, cut into strips

1 cup cornmeal

1 tablespoon sea salt or kosher salt

Ground black pepper to taste

½ cup olive oil, or more as needed

1½ cups Incredible Hollandaise Sauce (see recipe in Sauces, Stocks, and Special Additions)

2 tablespoons Parmesan cheese

Sprinkle of paprika (optional)

1. Preheat oven to 350°F.

2. Make sure the cooked broccoli is well drained. You can cook it in advance and place it in the refrigerator on paper towels.

3. Roll the chicken in the cornmeal; sprinkle with salt and pepper.

4. Heat the olive oil in a sauté pan. Sauté the chicken for 5 minutes on each side until golden brown, adding more oil if the pan gets dry.

5. Either butter a 2-quart casserole or prepare it with nonstick spray. Place the broccoli in the bottom and spoon some hollandaise over the top. Arrange the chicken over the broccoli and pour on the rest of the sauce. Sprinkle with Parmesan cheese and paprika. Bake for 30 minutes.

ELEGANT CHICKEN AND FRUIT-FILLED CORN CREPES

SERVES 4 | Calories: 557 | Protein: 28 grams | Carbohydrates: 57 grams | Fiber: 8 grams | Fat: 22 grams | Sodium: 181 milligrams

½ cup GF Homemade Chicken Stock (see recipe in Sauces, Stocks, and Special Additions)

1 tablespoon arrowroot

⅔ pound boneless, skinless chicken breasts

½ cup cornmeal

3 tablespoons unsalted butter

Salt to taste

2 teaspoons freshly ground black pepper

½ cup dried cranberries soaked in ⅔ cup apple juice or wine

¼ cup dried cherries soaked in ½ cup orange juice

¼ cup chopped celery tops

24 pearl onions (frozen is fine)

1 tablespoon rosemary leaves, dried and crumbled

½ cup apple brandy (such as Calvados)

8 large GF Crepes (see recipe in Sauces, Stocks, and Special Additions)

2 tablespoons butter, melted, or olive oil

1. Preheat oven to 350°F.

2. Mix the chicken stock and the arrowroot and set aside.

3. Dredge the chicken breasts in cornmeal and sauté them in 3 tablespoons butter over medium heat. Add the salt and pepper and the chicken stock/arrowroot mixture to the pan, stirring to make a sauce.

4. Add the soaked fruit, celery tops, onions, rosemary, and apple brandy. Cover and cook for 20 minutes over low heat.

5. Cool and remove the chicken from the pan. Cut it into small pieces and shred. Return the chicken and remaining liquid to the sauce. Divide the sauce among the 8 crepes. Roll the crepes, place them seam-side down in a greased baking dish, and drizzle with melted butter or olive oil. Heat them in the oven for 10–15 minutes. Serve over greens or sautéed spinach.

SPICY OLIVE CHICKEN

SERVES 4 | Calories: 418 | Protein: 53 grams | Carbohydrates: 8 grams | Fiber: 1 gram | Fat: 16 grams | Sodium: 634 milligrams

1 3-pound chicken, cut into 8 pieces

4 tablespoons unsalted butter

⅔ cup chopped sweet onion

½ cup GF Homemade Chicken Stock (see recipe in Sauces, Stocks, and Special Additions)

½ cup dry white wine

24 green olives, pitted

1 teaspoon prepared Dijon mustard

Salt, black pepper, and hot sauce to taste

½ cup capers

Fresh parsley, chopped, for garnish

1. Heat a medium-sized saucepan to medium-high heat.

2. Sprinkle the chicken pieces with salt and pepper and brown them in the butter. Sauté the onion in the same pan. Add the stock, wine, and olives.

3. Using a fork, whisk in the mustard. Cover the pan and simmer until the chicken is done, about 25 minutes. Add salt, pepper, capers, and hot sauce.

4. Pour sauce and olives over the chicken, mashed potatoes, rice, or rice noodles. Garnish with chopped parsley.

GET THE **EDGE**

Capers are flavorful berries. Picked green, they can be packed in salt or brine. Try to find the smallest—they seem to have more flavor than the big ones do. Capers are great on their own or incorporated into sauces. They are also good in salads and as a garnish on many dishes that would otherwise be dull.

TURKEY AND CILANTRO LETTUCE WRAPS

SERVES 4 | Calories: 523 | Protein: 40 grams | Carbohydrates: 10 grams | Fiber: 5 grams | Fat: 36 grams | Sodium: 161 milligrams

3 tablespoons olive oil

1 cup white onion (fine chopped)

1 pound ground turkey

4 garlic cloves (minced)

Salt and pepper to taste

1 cup fresh cilantro (fine chopped)

8 iceberg lettuce leaves

2 cups radish sprouts

2 ripe avocados (cut into small cubes)

1. Heat a medium-size sauté pan to medium-high heat. Add olive oil and onions and sauté until onions are opaque. Then mix in turkey. Add garlic, salt, and pepper, and blend ingredients into a mixture. After 2 minutes, turn off heat and blend in cilantro.

2. Open a lettuce leaf, fill with ⅛ the mixture, add ⅛ the radish sprouts, ⅛ the avocado cubes, and then roll the leaf closed. Repeat the process with the other leaves and serve.

GET THE **EDGE**

This recipe is made with cilantro—Chef Ross's favorite herb! It gives any food it is combined with an amazingly fresh flavor. Cilantro is also known as coriander leaves or Chinese parsley, and it tastes like a mixture of parsley and citrus flavors. This herb also acts as a cleansing agent and helps to remove heavy metals and toxins from the body. The oil can also help with digestion by producing digestive enzymes.

TURKEY-STUFFED CABBAGE ROLLS

SERVES 4 | Calories: 486 | Protein: 40 grams | Carbohydrates: 46 grams | Fiber: 9 grams | Fat: 15 grams | Sodium: 465 milligrams

2 8-ounce cans tomato juice

16 green cabbage leaves

1 pound ground turkey

1 cup white onion (chopped fine)

4 garlic cloves (minced)

1 cup white beans

4 tablespoons fresh thyme

1½ cups long grain white rice (cooked)

Salt and pepper to taste

1. Heat a medium-sized sauté pan to medium heat, then add the tomato juice and cabbage leaves. Cover and sauté for 4 minutes or until the leaves have softened. Remove the cabbage to a plate, leaving the tomato juice in the pan, and let the cabbage cool.

2. Lower heat under the sauté pan to lowest setting or low.

3. In a medium mixing bowl, combine turkey, onion, garlic, beans, thyme, rice, salt, and pepper.

4. Open a cabbage leaf and add $\frac{1}{8}$ of the turkey filling and roll closed.

5. Take a second leaf and wrap it around the filled cabbage leaf, fold in the corners, and roll the leaf until it's closed. Repeat this process with the other leaves, then place the rolls back in the sauté pan and cover. Raise the heat to medium low and cook for 18 minutes. Remove the rolls to a serving plate. Spoon a generous amount of the juice in the pan over the rolls and serve.

TURKEY PICCATA

SERVES 4 | Calories: 567 | Protein: 40 grams | Carbohydrates: 10 grams | Fiber: <1 gram | Fat: 40 grams | Sodium: 366 milligrams

2 boneless turkey breasts (butterflied and then cut in half)

Sea salt and pepper to taste

All-purpose gluten-free flour, for dredging

6 tablespoons unsalted butter

5 tablespoons extra-virgin olive oil

⅓ cup fresh lemon juice

½ cup GF Homemade Vegetable Stock (see recipe in Sauces, Stocks, and Special Additions)

¼ cup brined capers, rinsed

⅜ cup fresh parsley, chopped

1. Season turkey breast with salt and pepper. Then dredge turkey in flour and shake off excess.

2. In a large skillet over medium-high heat, melt 2 tablespoons of butter with 3 tablespoons olive oil. When butter and oil start to sizzle, add 2 pieces of turkey and cook for 3 minutes. When turkey is browned, flip and cook other side for 3 minutes. Remove and transfer to plate.

3. Melt 2 more tablespoons butter and add another 2 tablespoons olive oil. When butter and oil start to sizzle, add the other 2 pieces of turkey and brown both sides in same manner. Remove pan from heat and add turkey to the plate.

4. Add lemon juice, stock, and capers to the pan. Return to stove and bring to boil, scraping up brown bits from the pan for extra flavor. Check for seasoning. Return all the turkey to the pan and simmer for 5 minutes. Remove turkey to platter. Add remaining 2 tablespoons butter to sauce and whisk vigorously. Pour sauce over turkey and garnish with parsley.

GET THE **EDGE**

The lemon in this recipe aids with weight loss because it is an effective way to help eliminate toxins, clean internal waste, and boost energy levels. The gluten-free flour replaces the gluten-containing flour that is used in most turkey piccata recipes. When you are shopping for gluten-free flour, read the labels carefully. Check the fat content of the different brands and choose the flour with the lowest percentage of saturated fat.

MOROCCAN EGGPLANT AND TURKEY CASSEROLE

SERVES 4 | Calories: 564 | Protein: 35 grams | Carbohydrates: 39 grams | Fiber: 5 grams | Fat: 30 grams | Sodium: 448 milligrams

2 large eggplants, peeled and cut vertically into long, thin slices

Table salt

1 red onion, peeled and diced

4 cloves garlic, peeled and minced

¼ cup olive oil, plus more for sautéing

1¼ pounds very lean ground turkey

¼ teaspoon cinnamon

½ teaspoon ground coriander seeds

Juice of 1 lemon

½ cup golden raisins (sultanas)

½ cup dried apricots, chopped

1 cup crushed tomatoes, with their juice

10 fresh mint leaves, torn into small pieces

Salt and pepper to taste

Hot paprika or cayenne to taste

1 teaspoon cornstarch (if needed)

1. Preheat oven to 350°F.

2. Slice the eggplant and stack it with plenty of salt between the layers. Let it rest while you prepare the filling.

3. Sauté the onion and garlic in a tablespoon of olive oil. Add the turkey when the vegetables are soft.

4. Add the rest of the ingredients and cook, stirring until well blended. The apricots will absorb much of the liquid. If mixture is still very loose, sprinkle with a teaspoon of cornstarch. Cover and simmer for 15 minutes.

5. Drain any liquid from the eggplant and place one layer in a well-oiled 11" x 13" baking dish. Add some of the turkey mixture, distributing carefully. Keep making layers until you have one final layer of eggplant. Sprinkle with extra oil and bake for 45 minutes. Serve in wedges. The traditional accompaniment is rice.

GET THE EDGE

Eggplants come in a number of sizes, shapes, and colors. They all taste pretty much the same, but the larger ones may have bitter seeds. An old method of sweetening them up is to peel and cut an eggplant paper-thin, salt the slices on each side, and stack them on a plate, under a weight. Then, a lot of brown juice comes out, and the slices are sweet.

TURKEY LASAGNA

SERVES 8 | Calories: 601 | Protein: 36 grams | Carbohydrates: 35 grams | Fiber: 2 grams | Fat: 35 grams | Sodium: 2250 milligrams

3 tablespoons olive oil

1 large yellow onion (sliced and chopped medium)

1 pound mild Italian turkey sausage (removed from casings)

4 garlic cloves

2 tablespoons dried oregano

Salt and pepper to taste

16 ounces ricotta cheese

2 cups fresh basil (rough chopped)

4 cups Carly's Tomato Sauce (see recipe in Sauces, Stocks, and Special Additions)

9 GF pasta lasagna noodles (cooked "al dente" and drained)

16 ounces mozzarella cheese (sliced in ¼" slices)

1. Preheat oven to 375°F.

2. Heat a large sauté pan to medium-high heat. Add olive oil and onion. Sauté until onions are opaque.

3. Add the crumbled sausage to the sauté pan and cook for 2 minutes or until browned. Then add the garlic and oregano to the pan and blend. Salt and pepper the pan mixture to taste, cook for 1 minute, and remove from heat.

4. In a food processor, add the ricotta cheese and basil. Process these ingredients until completely blended or about 1 minute.

5. In a 13" x 9" Pyrex glass dish add a thin layer of sauce mixture. Place a layer of 3 noodles over the sauce mixture. Add a layer of the sauce mixture on top of the noodles. Place a layer of 3 more noodles on top of the sauce mixture. Using a soft rubber spatula, spread the ricotta cheese and basil mixture evenly on top of the second layer of noodles. Add the third layer of noodles on top of the cheese layer. Add the remainder of the sauce mixture on top of the third layer of noodles and cover with the sliced mozzarella cheese.

6. Place dish in the oven and bake for 25–30 minutes or until mozzarella is browned. Remove from oven, let rest for 5 minutes, and serve.

GET THE **EDGE**

Don't feel that you have to give up lasagna just because you are going gluten-free and trying to lose weight. The GF lasagna noodles are readily available in most health-food stores, and the turkey serves as a healthy, lower-fat replacement for the red meat that is typically used in this recipe. Serve this entrée with a small dinner salad for extra nutritional value.

GRILLED TURKEY BREAST SALAD WITH ROASTED RED PEPPER DRESSING

SERVES 4 | Calories: 249 | Protein: 19 grams | Carbohydrates: 13 grams | Fiber: 3 grams | Fat: 14 grams | Sodium: 198 milligrams

2 tablespoons canola oil

1 whole turkey breast (boneless, skinless)

1 tablespoon paprika

Salt and pepper to taste

1 18–ounce jar roasted red peppers (drained well)

½ cup soy mayonnaise

4 cups romaine lettuce (chopped fine)

2 cups grape tomatoes (washed, drained)

1 cucumber (peeled, cut into ¼" slices)

1. Heat a medium sauté pan to medium-high heat and add the oil.

2. Sprinkle the turkey breast with paprika, salt, and pepper, then sear for 2 minutes on each side.

3. Reduce heat to medium low and cover. Continue cooking for 15–18 minutes or completely cooked through. Remove to cool.

4. In a small mixing bowl add the red peppers and mayonnaise. Add salt and pepper; then, with a hand blender, blend until completely combined. Set aside.

5. Place the lettuce on a large salad bowl or plate and surround it along the edges with the tomatoes and cucumber. Slice the turkey into ¼"-wide slices and lay them evenly on top of the lettuce. Pour the red pepper dressing on top and serve.

BAKED TURKEY BREAST WITH CORN CAKE AND GF CRANBERRIES

SERVES 4 | Calories: 693 | Protein: 40 grams | Carbohydrates: 86 grams | Fiber: 6 grams | Fat: 22 grams | Sodium: 628 milligrams

2 tablespoons thyme (fresh, plus 4 sprigs for garnish)

1 tablespoon paprika

1 tablespoon cumin

1 tablespoon celery salt

Cracked black pepper to taste

Salt to taste

2 turkey breasts (boneless, skinless)

1 tablespoon canola oil

8 tablespoons soy butter (4 tablespoons for sautéing turkey, 4 tablespoons for corn cake)

2 cups yellow onion (chopped medium)

1 cup celery (chopped small)

¾ cup cornmeal

¼ cup water

2 tablespoons soy cream

½ teaspoon baking soda

1 cup dried cranberries

1 cup fresh corn (cut from the cobs)

1. Heat a large sauté pan to medium-high heat.

2. In a small mixing bowl, thoroughly combine 2 tablespoons thyme, paprika, cumin, celery salt, pepper, and salt. Coat the turkey with the mixture generously and set aside.

3. Add the oil to the pan and heat for 20 seconds, then add 4 tablespoons of butter and wait until it's completely melted. Add the turkey and sear on both sides for 3 minutes or nicely browned.

4. Turn heat down to low, add the onion and celery, and cover the pan. Cook for 15–18 minutes or until turkey is firm to the touch. The turkey will baste itself in the covered pan.

5. Meanwhile, preheat oven to 425°F.

6. Grease an 8" x 8" Pyrex baking pan well with canola spray. Add 4 tablespoons of butter and cornmeal into the medium mixing food processor bowl and blend for 30 seconds. Then add the water, cream, salt, and baking soda and blend for 30 seconds. Fold the dried cranberries and corn into the mixture.

7. Transfer mixture to the baking pan and bake for 10–12 minutes or until golden brown. Remove from the oven and place on a baking rack to cool. When cool enough, slice the corn cake into 8 squares.

8. Remove the turkey from the sauté pan and set aside to cool. Be sure to reserve the remaining contents of the pan. When cool enough, slice turkey into ¼" slices, place on a large serving platter, and pour the contents of the pan over the turkey. Arrange the 8 corn cakes around the edge of the platter, garnish with thyme sprigs, and serve.

GET THE **EDGE**

Healthy eating and weight loss are easier to accomplish once you begin to think about food as nourishment rather than something to just gulp down in between meetings or on the way to an appointment. It is important to slow down. Chew your food slowly and savor every bite. This way, you'll pay more attention to how you feel and will have a better idea of when to put down your fork.

ZUCCHINI BOATS WITH KING CRAB

SERVES 4 | Calories: 378 | Protein: 37 grams | Carbohydrates: 13 grams | Fiber: 3 grams | Fat: 16 grams | Sodium: 924 milligrams

4 medium-size zucchinis

3 tablespoons of butter

2 tablespoons extra-virgin olive oil

2 pounds (minimum) king crab legs and claws (broken up into pieces and cracked; do not remove from the shell)

1 bunch medium-size green onions (topped, sliced fine) plus a handful for garnish

3 garlic cloves, chopped fine

½ cup sherry

1. Halve each zucchini and scoop out the meat to create a boat. Set the zucchini meat aside.

2. Bring a medium-size sauté pan up to medium-high heat and add the butter and olive oil. Add the king crab and sauté for 2 minutes. Remove to a bowl to cool.

3. Add the green onions and garlic to the hot pan. As soon as the onions are opaque, add the zucchini meat. Sauté for 2 minutes and reserve to a small bowl.

4. Remove the crabmeat from the shells and add to the reserved zucchini mixture.

5. Either sauté the zucchini boats' bottoms on an indoor grill or keep the heat up on your sauté pan and cook them in the butter/oil remaining in the pan.

6. Drain the zucchini on paper towels and then mound the crab mixture on the boats.

7. Add the sherry to the sauté pan and burn off the alcohol. Pour liquid over the stuffed boats and sprinkle on a handful of chopped green onions to garnish.

GRILLED HALIBUT WITH GUACAMOLE

SERVES 4 | Calories: 695 | Protein: 67 grams | Carbohydrates: 5 grams | Fiber: 3 grams |
Fat: 44 grams | Sodium: 178 milligrams

2 cups cilantro (rough chopped; save a small amount chopped and a few leaves for garnish)

1 cup canola oil

Sea salt and pepper to taste

2 large avocados

2 tablespoons red onion (minced fine)

2 tablespoons lime juice

4 8-ounce fresh halibut fillets

2 limes (cut into wedges for garnish)

1. Heat an outdoor or indoor grill to medium-high heat for about 10 minutes.

2. Blend together cilantro and oil with a hand blender in a small bowl. Add salt and pepper and set aside.

3. To make guacamole, cut avocado in half and remove pit. With a spoon, remove the avocado meat to a small mixing bowl. Add onion and lime juice to the bowl and blend with avocado using a fork.

4. Lightly coat cilantro/oil mixture on the halibut fillets, then sprinkle a small amount of salt and pepper on top and bottom of the halibut. Place fillets on hot grill until lightly browned or to preferred doneness.

5. Place a generous dollop of guacamole on a serving plate with a sprinkle of cilantro on top. Place the halibut on the plate, add a slice of lime, garnish with cilantro leaves, and serve.

RED SNAPPER WITH MUSHROOMS AND WHITE WINE

SERVES 4 | Calories: 798 | Protein: 70 grams | Carbohydrates: 4 grams | Fiber: <1 gram | Fat: 45 grams | Sodium: 154 milligrams

Sea salt and pepper to taste

4 10-ounce red snapper fillets

Canola oil spray

2 cups large fresh whole white button mushrooms (sliced ¼" thick)

¾ cup olive oil

8 tablespoons butter

2 shallots, fine chopped

2 cups dry white wine like Sauvignon Blanc (Chardonnay will work but tastes sweeter)

6 sprigs of fresh thyme with leaves removed plus 4 for garnish or 2 teaspoons of dry thyme leaves

1 fresh lemon cut into ¼" slices

1. Heat an indoor or outdoor grill to medium-high temperature for ten minutes. Salt and pepper fillets to taste on both sides and gently spray with canola oil. Add fillets to grill and cook for 3 minutes per side or to desired doneness. Remove to serving platter.

2. Rinse mushrooms with water in a colander, rinse dry quickly with a paper towel, and set aside.

3. Heat a large sauté pan to medium-high heat. Add oil and butter and stir until butter is melted. Add mushrooms and chopped shallots. After 1 minute add salt and pepper.

4. After 2 more minutes add wine and thyme and cook down until liquid thickens. When finished, pour over grilled fish. Surround plate with lemon slices and 4 thyme sprigs, and serve.

GET THE EDGE

Most people who are trying to lose weight often focus on reducing portion sizes, but *what* you eat is actually more important than how much you eat. Processed foods might fill you up, but your body and metabolism have difficulty functioning properly fueled by foods with poor nutritional value. Red snapper and mushrooms are both unprocessed, natural foods that are quickly digested.

SEA BASS WITH AVOCADO AND CILANTRO-INFUSED OIL

SERVES 4 | Calories: 676 | Protein: 53 grams | Carbohydrates: 6 grams | Fiber: 4 grams | Fat: 46 grams | Sodium: 337 milligrams

Canola oil spray

Sea salt and pepper to taste

4 8-ounce Chilean sea bass fillets

1 cup fresh cilantro (rough chopped) plus 1 cup for garnish

1 cup canola oil

2 avocados (ripe, sliced into ¼" thin wedges)

1. Spray a large sauté pan with oil spray and bring to medium-high heat. Sprinkle sea salt and black pepper to taste on both sides of sea bass. Add to pan and sauté for 3 minutes per side or to preferred doneness. Remove sea bass and set aside.

2. Blend the cilantro and oil in food processor, blender, or in a bowl with a hand blender. Set aside.

3. Cut each avocado in half from the top to the bottom and remove pit. Cut halves in half. With skin intact, cut 4 vertical slices and then gently remove from skin.

4. Arrange avocado slices in a fan on serving plate. Place sea bass right below the fan. Make a circle around the sea bass with drops of the cilantro-infused oil. Garnish top of sea bass with cilantro leaves and serve.

TILAPIA WITH CRUNCHY CORN CRUST

SERVES 4 | Calories: 762 | Protein: 48 grams | Carbohydrates: 14 grams | Fiber: <1 gram | Fat: 56 grams | Sodium: 449 milligrams

2 cups cornmeal

Salt and pepper to taste

4 6-ounce fresh tilapia fillets

2 eggs (beaten)

1 tablespoon water

1 cup canola oil

1 stick soy butter

½ cups fresh thyme leaves (removed from stems)

1. Season cornmeal with salt and pepper. Place tilapia on one plate and cornmeal on another.

2. Crack the eggs into a small mixing bowl, add water, and blend together using a fork. Coat tilapia with cornmeal, then coat with egg. Then coat again with cornmeal and reserve to serving plate.

3. Heat a medium-size sauté pan to medium-high heat. Add canola oil to pan and heat for 2 minutes. When sauté pan is fully heated, add tilapia and sauté until golden brown on both sides or until desired doneness.

4. Meanwhile, bring a small saucepan to medium heat. Add butter, thyme leaves, salt, and pepper. Stir until butter is melted. Turn heat down to low and stir every 30 seconds until sauce reaches desired thickness.

5. Remove tilapia to serving plate, cover with butter and thyme sauce, and serve.

CRUNCHY BUTTERFLIED SHRIMP IN ORANGE SAUCE

SERVES 4 | Calories: 649 | Protein: 28 grams | Carbohydrates: 25 grams | Fiber: <1 gram | Fat: 48 grams | Sodium: 657 milligrams

20 jumbo shrimp (defrosted, tail on, peeled and deveined)

4 cups GF Panko-Style Bread Crumbs (see recipe in Sauces, Stocks, and Special Additions)

Salt and white pepper (black pepper optional)

2 eggs

6 tablespoons soy butter

1 large navel orange (zest removed, juice reserved)

8 green onions (fine chopped) plus 1 cup reserved for garnish

4 cloves garlic (minced)

1 tablespoon fresh gingerroot (minced)

1½ cup canola oil

1. With a sharp paring knife, butterfly the shrimp and set aside. Place crumbs on a separate plate right next to reserved shrimp and add salt and pepper.

2. In a small mixing bowl, completely blend the eggs. Coat each shrimp with the crumbs, then coat with egg, and coat with crumbs again. Set aside.

3. Heat a small saucepan to medium heat. Add the butter, orange juice, green onions, garlic, and gingerroot. Reduce until sauce thickens and turn heat to low.

4. Heat a medium-sized sauté pan to medium-high heat and add the oil. When the oil begins to ripple, add the shrimp and sauté until golden brown. Remove the shrimp to a plate lined with a paper towel and allow excess oil to drain off for 1 minute.

5. Place the shrimp on a serving plate and cover with orange sauce. Sprinkle orange zest and green onion on top of the shrimp and serve.

CRAB CAKES LE ROI WITH MANGO SALSA

SERVES 4 | Calories: 429 | Protein: 27 grams | Carbohydrates: 35 grams | Fiber: 4 grams | Fat: 20 grams | Sodium: 1111 milligrams

FOR CRAB CAKES:

32 ounces crabmeat (of your choice)

2 cups cornmeal

1 cup green onions (fine chopped)

1 cup cilantro (fine chopped)

1 fresh lemon (cut in half)

1 cup low-fat Thousand Island dressing

Salt and pepper to taste

1 cup canola oil

4 cups romaine lettuce (rough chopped)

FOR SALSA:

2 Roma tomatoes (diced)

1 cup mango (diced)

1 cup cilantro (fine chopped)

1 cup red onion (chopped medium)

1. Preheat oven to 425°F

2. In a large mixing bowl, combine crabmeat, cornmeal, green onions, cilantro, 2 tablespoons lemon juice, ¾ cup Thousand Island dressing, salt, and pepper.

3. Take a handful of the mixture and, with wet hands, form into 8 3"-diameter cakes and set on a plate. Cover with plastic wrap and let set in the fridge for 20–30 minutes. Coat again with cornmeal before sautéing.

4. Add canola oil to a medium sauté pan and heat to medium-high heat. Add crab cakes and sauté until both sides are golden brown.

5. Place sauté pan in the oven for 10–12 minutes.

6. Meanwhile, make salsa: In a small mixing bowl, place tomatoes, mango, cilantro, red onion, and 1 tablespoon lemon juice and combine. Salt and pepper the salsa to taste.

7. Cover a serving plate with lettuce. In the middle of the plate, spoon the salsa on top of the lettuce evenly. Set cakes on top of the salsa and spoon a generous dollop of Thousand Island dressing on each cake. Garnish with a lemon wedge and serve.

GET THE **EDGE**

Some people prefer to avoid grains in their diet. Although that's not necessary, we use a corn-based flour here to achieve a completely grain-free recipe. Corn flour is milled from corn into a fine, white powder, and is used for thickening recipes and sauces. Corn flour is very low in fat and easy to cook with as it resembles wheat flour in its texture and it has a great flavor.

HALIBUT CHINOISE

SERVES 4 | Calories: 467 | Protein: 51 grams | Carbohydrates: 41 grams | Fiber: 2 grams | Fat: 9 grams | Sodium: 1297 milligrams

2 cups Panko-Style Bread Crumbs (see recipe in Sauces, Stocks, and Special Additions)

Salt and cracked black pepper to taste

2 eggs

1 teaspoon water

4 6-ounce fresh halibut fillets

1 cup GF hoisin sauce

4 green onions (fine chopped, reserve 1 tablespoon for garnish)

4 garlic cloves (minced)

2 tablespoons fresh thyme

1. Preheat over to 425°F.

2. Place crumbs on a plate and add salt and pepper.

3. Crack the eggs in a small mixing bowl, add a teaspoon of water, blend with a fork, and place next to the plate of crumbs.

4. Coat the halibut with crumbs and then coat with egg. Then coat again with crumbs.

5. Place halibut on a baking sheet covered in tin foil. Place baking sheet in the oven and bake for 15–18 minutes or until golden brown. Remove to serving plate.

6. In a small saucepan, on medium heat, add the hoisin sauce, green onion, garlic, and thyme. Stir until combined and simmer for 3 minutes. Turn heat to low. Cover halibut with sauce, sprinkle with green onions, and serve.

SALMON CROQUETTE LETTUCE WRAP

SERVES 4 | Calories: 533 | Protein: 45 grams | Carbohydrates: 13 grams | Fiber: 3 grams | Fat: 32 grams | Sodium: 338 milligrams

24 ounces salmon (cooked and flaked or canned)

1 cup red onion (fine chopped)

1 cup roasted red pepper (fine chopped)

3 teaspoons garlic powder

½ cup Basic Aioli (see recipe in Sauces, Stocks, and Special Additions)

3 tablespoons fresh thyme leaves

2 teaspoons lemon juice

Salt and pepper to taste

16 iceberg lettuce leaves

2 cups radish sprouts

1. In a medium-sized mixing bowl add salmon, onion, red pepper, garlic powder, aioli, thyme, lemon juice, salt, and pepper. Fold mixture until completely combined.

2. Open a lettuce leaf, fill with ⅛ of the mixture, add ⅛ of the radish sprouts, and roll the leaf closed. Repeat with the other leaves and serve.

WHITE CLAM PIZZA

SERVES 4 | Calories: 638 | Protein: 30 grams | Carbohydrates: 62 grams | Fiber: 7 grams | Fat: 19 grams | Sodium: 528 milligrams

1 GF Cornmeal Pizza Crust (see recipe in Sauces, Stocks, and Special Additions)

2 8-ounce cans chopped littleneck clams

2 cloves of garlic, chopped fine

1 cup sweet basil (chiffonade or thinly sliced)

*Eggless option: Combine 2 tablespoons flaxseed meal and 6 tablespoons water; let stand one minute. Add to recipe as you would the eggs.

1. Preheat oven to 425°F.
2. Prepare GF Cornmeal Pizza Crust and cover with clams, garlic, basil, and olive oil. Bake for 15–18 minutes.

GET THE **EDGE**

The pizza dough in this recipe can be stored in the refrigerator for a few days. Wrap it in plastic wrap and store in plastic bag. When you're ready to bake, take dough out of refrigerator and allow to rest 30 minutes before following the recipe instructions.

SHRIMP PAD THAI

SERVES 4 | Calories: 385 | Protein: 22 grams | Carbohydrates: 41 grams | Fiber: 2 grams | Fat: 14 grams | Sodium: 1206 milligrams

16 ounces Thai rice noodles

¾ tablespoon tamarind paste

¼ cup hot water

3 tablespoons fish sauce

3 tablespoons brown sugar

¼ cup roasted peanuts

½ cup fresh cilantro

3 tablespoons canola oil

1 shallot (minced)

4 garlic cloves

3 cups 31–40 size raw shrimp (defrosted, deveined, shelled)

3 tablespoons GF Homemade Chicken Stock (see recipe in Sauces, Stocks, and Special Additions)

1 egg

2 cups bean sprouts

1. Bring a large pot of water to boil, then remove from heat. Add the rice noodles. Soak noodles until al dente.

2. Drain and rinse the noodles thoroughly with cold water, then set aside.

3. Make the pad thai sauce: In a small bowl or cup, dissolve the tamarind paste in the hot water. Then add the fish sauce, sugar, peanuts, and cilantro, stirring well. (Add as much or as little fish sauce as you prefer, but don't skimp on the sugar; it is needed to balance out the sourness of the tamarind.) Set aside.

4. Warm a wok or large frying pan over medium-high heat. Add 2 tablespoons oil and the shallots and garlic. Stir-fry for 1 minute.

5. Add the shrimp plus 2–3 tablespoons chicken stock. Stir-fry 2–3 minutes, or until shrimp are pink and plump.

6. Push ingredients to the side of the wok/pan, making room in the center. Add another tablespoon of oil, then crack in the egg. Stir-fry to scramble (30 seconds to 1 minute).

7. Add the drained noodles and drizzle the pad thai sauce over the top. Gently toss everything together.

8. Stir-fry 4–6 minutes, or until noodles are a little bit sticky. Serve.

FISH STICKS ENSENADA STYLE WITH COLESLAW

SERVES 4 | Calories: 663 | Protein: 65 grams | Carbohydrates: 52 grams | Fiber: 3 grams | Fat: 19 grams | Sodium: 1140 milligrams

4 cups GF Panko-Style Bread Crumbs (see recipe in Sauces, Stocks, and Special Additions)

2 eggs (plus 1 tablespoon of water, beaten and combined well)

4 8-ounce cod fillets (cut into 3" x 1" "sticks")

1 bag shredded coleslaw (premade)

1 tablespoon cumin

1 tablespoon celery salt

Cracked black pepper to taste

1 cup soy mayonnaise

2 cups cilantro (fresh, chopped fine; reserve ½ cup for garnish)

1 lemon (cut into 4 wedges)

Canola spray

1. Preheat oven to 425°F.

2. Put bread crumbs on a large plate and eggs in a medium mixing bowl.

3. Coat a piece of fish with egg, then coat with bread crumbs, and place on a foil-lined and oiled baking sheet. Repeat this process until all fish pieces are breaded.

4. Place baking sheet in the oven for 20–25 minutes or until "sticks" are golden brown. Then remove and set aside.

5. In a medium-size mixing bowl add the coleslaw, cilantro, cumin, celery salt, pepper, and mayonnaise. Stir with a large spoon or fork until combined well and set aside.

6. Place a generous amount of the coleslaw mixture on each plate, and top with fish sticks. Sprinkle cilantro on top, garnish with a lemon wedge, and serve.

CRAB-STUFFED SOLE

SERVES 4 | Calories: 934 | Protein: 76 grams | Carbohydrates: 10 grams | Fiber: <1 gram | Fat: 64 grams | Sodium: 1071 milligrams

1 cup soy butter

½ cup leek (sliced ¼" thick)

1 tablespoon lemon juice

Salt and pepper to taste

1 cup parsley (chopped fine)

1 cup soy mayonnaise

2 cups crabmeat (fresh or canned)

1 cup bay shrimp (defrosted)

4 8-ounce sole fillets (wild; fresh, not frozen)

Canola oil spray

4 toothpicks

1 cup soy mozzarella cheese

1 lemon (cut into wedges)

1. Preheat the oven to 375°F.

2. Heat a large sauté pan to medium heat. Add the butter and heat for 20 seconds, then add the leek. Sauté for 1 minute and then add the lemon juice, salt, pepper, parsley, and mayonnaise. Stir until completely blended.

3. Add the crabmeat and shrimp and gently fold into the mixture with a wooden spoon or spatula. Turn off heat and cover.

4. Place the fillets on a large foil-lined baking sheet sprayed with oil and sprinkle each fillet with a pinch of salt.

5. Place a generous dollop of the crabmeat mixture on the bottom ⅓ of each fillet. Then, while gently holding the lower ⅓ of the fillet, fold the other end over the mixture and seal with a toothpick. Generously sprinkle with cheese and bake for 15–18 minutes, or until the cheese is lightly browned. Garnish with lemon wedges and serve.

LIME SHRIMP STIR-FRY

SERVES 4 | Calories: 497 | Protein: 44 grams | Carbohydrates: 40 grams | Fiber: 3 grams | Fat: 16 grams | Sodium: 1396 milligrams

1½ pounds shrimp (21–25 size, peeled, deveined, defrosted)

3 garlic cloves (minced)

½ cup rice wine vinegar

4 tablespoons canola oil (2 for marinade and 2 for sauté)

3 medium limes (halved and juiced)

1 cup cilantro (fresh, rough chopped)

Salt and pepper to taste

4 green onions (cut 1" long on bias)

1 can baby ears of corn (cut into 1" pieces)

2 cups snow peas

1 can water chestnuts

4 cups bean sprouts

½ cup tamari

2 cups jasmine rice (cooked)

1. In a large sealable plastic bag, combine the shrimp, 2 cloves of minced garlic, vinegar, 2 tablespoons oil, lime juice, ½ of the cilantro, salt, and pepper. Let marinate in the refrigerator for 30 minutes to an hour.

2. Heat a large sauté pan to medium-high heat. Add 2 tablespoons of the oil to the pan and heat for 45 seconds, then add the shrimp and marinade, 1 clove minced garlic, onions, remaining cilantro, corns, peas, and chestnuts. Sauté for 2 minutes and add the bean sprouts and tamari. Stir-fry until the shrimp are pink.

3. Place the rice on a large serving plate, cover with the shrimp stir-fry mixture, and serve.

SALMON CROQUETTES

SERVES 4 | Calories: 489 | Protein: 37 grams | Carbohydrates: 24 grams | Fiber: 2 grams | Fat: 26 grams | Sodium: 842 milligrams

3 tablespoons canola oil

1 pound fresh salmon

1 cup GF Panko-Style Bread Crumbs (see recipe in Sauces, Stocks, and Special Additions)

2 eggs

3 green onions (chopped medium), reserve 1 for garnish

2 garlic cloves (minced fine)

2 tablespoons Homemade GF Mayonnaise (see recipe in Sauces, Stocks, and Special Additions)

1 lemon (juiced, zest removed and set aside)

1 teaspoon cayenne pepper

Salt and black pepper to taste

2 tablespoons fat-free Thousand Island dressing

1. Heat a large sauté pan to medium heat and add the canola oil.

2. In a large mixing bowl, add the salmon, ½ cup of bread crumbs, eggs, onions, garlic, mayonnaise, 1 tablespoon of lemon zest, 2 tablespoons of lemon juice, cayenne, salt, and pepper. Combine with a fork until completely mixed.

3. Make 8 equal-size cakes, roll in remaining bread crumbs, and add to the pan.

4. Sauté the cakes for 3–4 minutes per side or until golden brown. Remove to a plate lined with paper towels to drain the excess oil.

5. When drained, place cakes on serving plate, drizzle some Thousand Island dressing on each, garnish with green onion, and serve.

GET THE **EDGE**

We prefer using wild salmon because it has less parasite danger and lower contaminant levels. In addition, farmed fish tends to have a higher fat content.

GRILLED SOLE WITH PURÉED PARSNIPS

SERVES 4 | Calories: 505 | Protein: 54 grams | Carbohydrates: 38 grams | Fiber: 8 grams | Fat: 14 grams | Sodium: 331 milligrams

6 large parsnips (peeled, cut into 1" pieces)

4 tablespoons soy butter

8 sprigs thyme (fresh, leaves removed, stems discarded) plus 4 sprigs for garnish

Salt and pepper to taste

8 sole fillets (fresh, not frozen)

Canola spray

GET THE **EDGE**

The sweet and soft flavor of the parsnips in this recipe complements the sole and makes a light dish taste rich without adding any fat. Parsnips resemble carrots but are lighter in color and deeper in flavor.

1. Heat a medium saucepan to medium-high heat, then add parsnips and salt and enough water to cover them. Cover the pan and bring the water to a boil then turn down to medium heat. Cook the parsnips for 25 minutes or until fork-tender.

2. Drain the water from the pan and add the butter and thyme leaves. Let the butter melt, then add salt and pepper. Purée the mixture with a hand blender and set aside.

3. Heat a griddle or large sauté pan to medium-high heat.

4. On a serving plate, lay out all the sole fillets and spray both sides with canola oil. Sprinkle salt on both sides of the fillets and place fillets on the griddle or in the pan. Sauté until lightly browned on both sides, then remove the fillets to a large serving plate.

5. Place a generous spoonful of the parsnip purée on each individual serving plate and flatten.

6. Place 2 fillets on top of the purée on each plate, garnish with a thyme sprig, and serve.

SEAFOOD MOUSSELINE STUFFED PORTOBELLO MUSHROOMS

SERVES 4 | Calories: 361 | Protein: 16 grams | Carbohydrates: 19 grams | Fiber: 1 gram | Fat: 25 grams | Sodium: 330 milligrams

½ pound small shrimp (tails off, peeled, deveined, defrosted)

½ pound fish (fresh sole, cod, snapper, halibut, or pollock)

1 egg (beaten)

1 pint soy cream

2 tablespoons basil (fresh, chopped fine)

2 garlic cloves (minced fine)

1 teaspoon lemon juice

Salt and pepper to taste

Canola oil spray

4 large portobello mushrooms (stem removed, inside scraped clean)

4 tablespoons soy or regular unsalted butter

2 shallots (minced fine)

1. Preheat oven to 400°F.

2. Add the shrimp, fish, egg, cream, basil, garlic, lemon juice, salt, and pepper to food processor bowl. To make the mousseline, pulse the processor until mixture is just well blended. Remove the bowl from the processor and set aside.

3. Line a baking sheet with foil and spray it with canola oil. Add the mushrooms, top side down, and fill them generously with the mousseline. Bake for 15–18 minutes or until just barely browned. Remove from oven to a large serving plate.

4. Heat a small sauté pan to medium heat. Add the butter, shallots, salt, and pepper to the pan. Cook for 3 minutes or until shallots are opaque but not browned. Spoon a generous amount of the shallot sauce over each mushroom and serve.

GET THE **EDGE**

The mushrooms in this dish contain a wide range of amino acids, which help with weight loss by ensuring that your body metabolizes energy properly. They also help your brain realize whether you are hungry or full.

SPAGHETTI SQUASH WITH CREAMY VODKA AND SHRIMP SAUCE

SERVES 6 | Calories: 397 | Protein: 28 grams | Carbohydrates: 35 grams | Fiber: 6 grams | Fat: 12 grams | Sodium: 708 milligrams

1 large (4 to 5 pounds) spaghetti squash, cooked

2 minced shallots

2 tablespoons olive oil

1 tablespoon butter

1 tablespoon arrowroot

½ cup vodka

1 28-ounce can crushed tomatoes

1 cup soy cream

1½ pounds shrimp, peeled and deveined

Salt and plenty of freshly ground pepper to taste

½ cup each chopped fresh parsley and basil

1. Place the cooked squash in a large bowl and keep warm while you make the sauce.

2. Sauté the minced shallots in a mixture of oil and butter. When soft, add the arrowroot. Cook and stir over low heat until well blended, then add the vodka and tomatoes.

3. Cover and simmer gently for 20 minutes.

4. Stir in the cream and heat slowly, then add the shrimp. Do not boil after the cream has been added. When the shrimp turns pink, pour with the sauce over the spaghetti squash, and add salt and pepper. Garnish with parsley and basil.

GET THE **EDGE**

To cook spaghetti squash, just cut it in half, and steam it in butter and a pinch of salt in the microwave for 5 minutes on high heat in a covered container.

POACHED LOBSTER IN CAPER BUTTER SAUCE

SERVES 4 | Calories: 448 | Protein: 51 grams | Carbohydrates: 23 grams | Fiber: 5 grams | Fat: 15 grams | Sodium: 815 milligrams

1½ pounds lobster, cut into 4 serving pieces

½ cup garbanzo flour

2 tablespoons olive oil

¼ cup dry white wine

¼ cup GF Homemade Chicken Stock (see recipe in Sauces, Stocks, and Special Additions)

1 tablespoon butter

2 tablespoons capers

Salt and pepper to taste

Paprika and lemon wedges for garnish

1. Dredge the lobster in flour, then sauté over medium heat in olive oil. Turn after 4 minutes.

2. Add the wine, stock, butter and capers. Simmer (poach) for about 8 minutes, or until the fish is cooked through. Place lobster on a warm plate, reduce sauce by half, and pour over lobster.

3. Sprinkle with salt, pepper, and paprika. Serve with lemon wedges.

SEAFOOD À LA KING

SERVES 4 | Calories: 366 | Protein: 30 grams | Carbohydrates: 22 grams | Fiber: 3 grams | Fat: 17 grams | Sodium: 594 milligrams

½ cup shallots, minced

¼ cup unsalted butter

20 small white mushrooms, cut in half

20 pearl onions, fresh or frozen, cut in half

2 tablespoons arrowroot

2 ounces cold water

1 tablespoon tomato paste

2 tablespoons brandy

1½ cups soy cream

Salt and pepper to taste

½ pound shrimp, cleaned and deveined

½ pound bay scallops

2 tablespoons red salmon caviar for garnish

1. Sauté the shallots in the butter over moderate heat for 5 minutes. Add the mushrooms and pearl onions. Stir, cooking for a few more minutes.

2. Mix the arrowroot with cold water and add to the pan, stirring to blend. Blend in the tomato paste and brandy. Warm the cream slightly, then stir it into the sauce in the pan. (You can prepare this dish in advance up to this point. Store in the refrigerator until ready to serve.)

3. Reheat the sauce but do not boil. Taste for salt and pepper and add the shrimp and scallops. When the shrimp turns pink, the dish is done. Garnish with caviar and serve.

GET THE **EDGE**

This dish was created at the Brighton Beach Hotel on Long Island, New York, by Chef George Greenwald for his boss, E. Clarke King, II. It became very popular when Campbell's came out with canned cream of mushroom soup, which was then often used as a base.

MUSSELS MARINIERE

SERVES 4 | Calories: 533 | Protein: 55 grams | Carbohydrates: 26 grams | Fiber: <1 gram | Fat: 18 grams | Sodium: 1087 milligrams

½ cup finely chopped onion

2 tablespoons butter

2 tablespoons arrowroot

1 cup dry white wine

½ cup celery tops, chopped

3 to 4 pounds mussels, scrubbed and tapped

1 cup soy cream

Salt and pepper to taste

Juice of ½ lemon

½ cup fresh Italian flat-leaf parsley, rinsed and chopped

1. Sauté the onion in the butter until soft. Work in the arrowroot. Whisk in the white wine and add the celery tops. Mix and bring to a boil.

2. Pour in the prepared mussels. Cover and continue to boil. After two minutes, stir to bring the bottom ones up.

3. Place a large serving bowl on the side of the pot. Remove mussels as they open.

4. When all of the mussels are open and removed from the pot, reduce heat and add the cream. Heat but do not boil. Add salt and pepper.

5. Pour sauce over the mussels; sprinkle with lemon juice and parsley. Serve in warm bowls with a big bowl for discarding the shells.

GET THE **EDGE**

Even the tastiest of mollusks and crustaceans love to be dipped or bathed in sauces—all gluten-free of course. And there are a variety of options and substitutions. Any citrus can be substituted for just about any other—for example, limes for lemons, grapefruit for orange—and you can blend them together for intriguing outcomes using your own original flair for flavors. Throw in some ginger, curry powder, or mustard and you'll add another layer of flavor.

LOBSTER WITH SHERRY SAUCE

SERVES 4 TO 6 | Calories: 557 | Protein: 64 grams | Carbohydrates: 11 grams | Fiber: 0 grams | Fat: 15 grams | Sodium: 723 milligrams

4 small lobsters, 1–1¼ pounds each

1 teaspoon GF Asian five-spice powder

1 clove garlic, minced

¼ cup sesame seed oil

¼ cup sherry

Juice of ½ lemon

2 tablespoons minced gingerroot

1. Preheat the broiler to 500°F.

2. Bring water in a 3–5 gallon lobster pot to a boil. Add the lobsters and boil for 20 minutes, then remove from pot, split them, and crack the claws.

3. Mix the rest of the ingredients together in a saucepan to make the sauce. Bring to a boil and spoon over the lobsters.

4. Broil for 3 minutes. Serve.

CURRIED SHRIMP WITH AVOCADOS

SERVES 4 | Calories: 741 | Protein: 18 grams | Carbohydrates: 20 grams | Fiber: 14 grams | Fat: 69 grams | Sodium: 359 milligrams

¾ cup Homemade GF Mayonnaise (see recipe in Sauces, Stocks, and Special Additions)

2 teaspoons curry powder

Juice of 1 lime

1 teaspoon hot chili oil or hot pepper sauce such as Tabasco

½ pound raw medium shrimp, peeled and deveined

4 ripe avocados, halved, peeled, and pitted

Hungarian sweet or hot paprika to taste

Dry-roasted peanuts, for garnish

1. Preheat oven to 350°F.

2. Mix the mayonnaise with the curry, lime juice, and hot chili oil. Chop the shrimp and mix it with the mayonnaise sauce.

3. Place the avocado halves in a baking dish coated with nonstick spray. Spoon the shrimp and sauce mixture into the avocados. Sprinkle with paprika and peanuts.

4. Bake the shrimp-stuffed avocados for 20 minutes. You can vary this by adding chopped tart apple, pineapple, or red grapes.

LENTILS AND CABBAGE

SERVES 4 | Calories: 360 | Protein: 9 grams | Carbohydrates: 23 grams | Fiber: 7 grams | Fat: 26 grams | Sodium: 146 milligrams

½ pound lentils

4 tablespoons unsalted butter

1 cup fresh white button mushrooms (chopped medium)

1 tablespoon oregano

1 tablespoon white balsamic vinegar

4 tablespoons canola oil

1 cup red onion (sliced thin)

1 head fresh green cabbage (cut into slaw)

Salt and pepper to taste

1. In a medium pan, add the lentils and cover with water. Cover pan, then bring to a boil. Once boiling, lower to a simmer and open cover enough to let steam out. Cook about 15–20 minutes or until soft. Remove from heat.

2. Heat a medium sauté pan to medium heat and add butter. Once butter has melted, add mushrooms, oregano, and vinegar. Sauté for 5 minutes or until mushrooms are cooked through. Add mushroom mixture to cooked lentils and blend.

3. Bring the sauté pan back to medium-high heat and add the canola oil. Add the onions and sauté until opaque. Then add the cabbage, salt, and pepper and sauté the cabbage and onions for 4 minutes, or until the cabbage is cooked through.

4. Transfer the cabbage mixture to the middle of a serving plate. Make a crater in the middle of the cabbage mixture, spoon the lentils in the crater, and serve.

VEGETARIAN SPAGHETTI AND "MEATBALLS"

SERVES 4 | Calories: 240 | Protein: 3 grams | Carbohydrates: 24 grams | Fiber: 6 grams | Fat: 16 grams | Sodium: 498 milligrams

1 large eggplant, peeled

¼ cup extra-virgin olive oil

2 whole spaghetti squash

Sea salt and pepper

2 cups Roma tomatoes (diced)

¼ cup fresh sweet basil (sliced into thin strands, then chopped)

1. Peel the eggplant and cut into balls using a large melon balling tool.

2. Bring the oil to medium-high heat in a large sauté pan. Add eggplant balls to pan and cook until golden brown. Set aside on paper towels.

3. Split the squashes in half and scrape out seeds. Season the spaghetti squash with olive oil, salt, and pepper. Place on a plate and microwave on high for 7 minutes. Remove and let rest until cool enough to handle.

4. When squash is cool enough to handle, use a large kitchen fork to scrape the strands of squash from the inside of the skin. Toss the spaghetti squash in the pan with the tomatoes and the eggplant "meatballs" just long enough to heat through. Sprinkle with basil and serve.

BROCCOLINI AND MUSHROOM CREPES

SERVES 4 | Calories: 293 | Protein: 13 grams | Carbohydrates: 23 grams | Fiber: 6 grams | Fat: 17 grams | Sodium: 275 milligrams

4 tablespoons unsalted butter or soy butter

1 cup white button mushrooms (cut into ¼" slices)

2 cups fresh broccolini (chopped medium)

2 garlic cloves (minced fine)

1 tablespoon lemon zest

4 GF Crepes (see recipe in Sauces, Stocks, and Special Additions)

1. Melt butter in a medium saucepan over medium heat. Add mushrooms and broccolini to the hot pan. Sauté for about 3 minutes or until tender. Add the garlic and lemon zest and continue to sauté for 1 minute. Remove vegetable mixture to a small bowl.

2. Lay a crepe on a serving plate, and spoon half the vegetable mixture onto the lower third of the crepe. Fold the bottom of the crepe over the mixture and then roll up the crepe completely. Repeat the process with the other crepes and serve.

RAINBOW VEGETABLE PLATE

SERVES 4 | Calories: 515 | Protein: 17 grams | Carbohydrates: 70 grams | Fiber: 12 grams | Fat: 18 grams | Sodium: 241 milligrams

8 tablespoons unsalted butter or soy butter

2 butternut squash (halved, seeds and pulp removed)

1 teaspoon ground cinnamon

1 teaspoon fresh nutmeg (grated fine)

4 tablespoons honey

16 baby carrots

6 sprigs fresh thyme

2 golden beets (leaves removed and peeled)

2 red beets (leaves removed and peeled)

2 8-ounce cans cannellini beans (drained well)

3 cloves garlic (minced fine)

1 cup water

24 ounces fresh spinach

Salt and black pepper to taste

1. Melt 2 tablespoons of the butter in the microwave for 15 seconds or until melted.

2. Place the squash halves in larger microwavable dish. Sprinkle squash with cinnamon and nutmeg. Drizzle honey and then the melted butter over the top of the squash. Microwave for 8 minutes or until soft. Remove from microwave but keep covered to retain heat.

3. Add the baby carrots to a small microwavable dish. Add 2 tablespoons of butter and 2 sprigs of thyme leaves. Microwave for 2 minutes and then keep covered to retain the heat.

4. Cut golden and red beets into bite-sized pieces and place in microwavable dish with 1 tablespoon of butter. Microwave for 2 minutes or until tender. Keep covered to retain the heat.

5. Heat a small saucepan to medium-high heat. Add the beans, ½ of the minced garlic, 2 tablespoons of butter, and 4 sprigs of thyme leaves. Heat for 4 minutes. Remove from the heat and cover to retain the heat.

6. Heat a medium sauté pan to medium-high heat. Add the water and bring to a boil. Add the spinach leaves and cook until spinach is completely wilted and the water is almost completely evaporated.

7. Reduce the heat to low, add 1 tablespoon of butter, remaining garlic, salt, and pepper. Cook for 2 minutes and remove to a large serving plate.

8. Place squash to the side of the spinach. Spoon beans into cavity of squash. Arrange carrots and red and golden beets evenly around the circumference of the serving plate, and serve.

TOFU WITH VEGETABLES AND THAI PEANUT SAUCE

SERVES 4 | Calories: 723 | Protein: 34 grams | Carbohydrates: 23 grams | Fiber: 8 grams | Fat: 58 grams | Sodium: 450 milligrams

1 cup coconut milk (shaken before adding)

5 tablespoons GF peanut butter

3 green onions (fine chopped)

1 tablespoon rice wine vinegar

1 tablespoon tamari

1 tablespoon lime zest or Thai lime (kaffir) leaves (fine chopped)

½ cup fresh cilantro

2 teaspoons Thai red curry sauce

Salt and pepper to taste

1 cup fresh peanuts (shelled and fine chopped)

3 tablespoons canola oil

2 blocks of pressed tofu (cut into 2" cubes)

2 cups snap peas

2 cups bean sprouts

1 cup red bell pepper (1" x ¼" strips)

1. Heat a medium sauté pan to medium-low heat, then add coconut milk, peanut butter, onions, vinegar, tamari, lime zest/kaffir leaves, cilantro, curry sauce, salt, pepper, and peanuts. Cook until just barely bubbling hot but not boiling. When the sauce comes to heat, immediately reduce the heat to low.

2. Heat a large sauté pan to medium-high heat. Add oil and sauté tofu cubes until lightly browned. Add the peas, sprouts, and red peppers to the pan and continue to sauté for 2 minutes.

3. Transfer the vegetable mixture to a large serving plate, cover with the sauce, and serve.

CORN CRUST PIZZA

SERVES 4 | Calories: 701 | Protein: 21 grams | Carbohydrates: 26 grams | Fiber: 6 grams | Fat: 58 grams | Sodium: 217 milligrams

1 GF Cornmeal Pizza Crust (see recipe in Sauces, Stocks, and Special Additions)

1 cup white button mushrooms (fresh, cut into ¼" slices)

1 cup Roma tomatoes (small dice)

1 cup fresh basil leaves (stack, rolled, sliced thinly into ribbons)

12 ounces shredded soy mozzarella cheese

2 tablespoons oregano (dried)

1. Preheat oven to 425°F.

2. Prepare GF Corn Meal Pizza Crust.

3. After removing crust from the oven, add the mushrooms, tomatoes, basil, cheese, and oregano toppings evenly. Distribute the ¾ cup olive oil evenly over the toppings without saturating the dough.

4. Return the baking sheet to the oven and bake for 12–15 minutes or until the cheese is bubbling and lightly browned. Remove the baking sheet from the oven and let cool for 3 minutes. Cut the pizza into 8 even slices and serve.

SAUCES, STOCKS, AND SPECIAL ADDITIONS

The benefits of making your own sauces, stocks, and special recipe ingredients are that you'll consume less processed food and you can also prevent the gluten contamination that may occur in store-bought foods. These special additions can be made in larger quantities for storing and freezing for future use.

SAUCES, STOCKS, AND SPECIAL ADDITIONS CONTENTS

SIDNEY'S GF BBQ SAUCE

MAKES 2 CUPS | Calories: 44 | Protein: <1 gram | Carbohydrates: 10 grams | Fiber: <1 gram | Fat: <1 gram | Sodium: 231 milligrams

¼ cup apple cider vinegar

½ cup water

½ cup GF ketchup (such as Annie's Naturals brand)

1 tablespoon molasses

1 tablespoon raw brown sugar

1 tablespoon chili powder

1 medium onion (chopped and sautéed until opaque)

1 tablespoon garlic powder

1 teaspoon ground coffee

Salt and pepper to taste

1. Heat a medium sauce pot to medium heat.
2. Add the vinegar, water, and ketchup and combine well.
3. Add all the remaining ingredients to the pot.
4. While stirring well, bring sauce to a simmer and reduce heat to low. Simmer for 30 minutes, let cool, and transfer to a reusable container.

ITALIAN-STYLE GF BREAD CRUMBS

MAKES 4 CUPS | Calories: 68 | Protein: 2 grams | Carbohydrates: 12 grams | Fiber: 1 gram | Fat: 1 gram | Sodium: 200 milligrams

1 loaf of certified GF bread (cut up into 2" cubes)

2 tablespoons fresh basil (fine chopped)

2 tablespoons oregano (dried)

1 tablespoon garlic powder

Salt and pepper to taste

1. Add the bread cubes to the bowl of the food processor and pulse 10 times or until fine.

2. Add remaining ingredients. Pulse 10 more times.

3. Remove to a reusable container to use or store for 2 months.

HOMEMADE GF MAYONNAISE

MAKES 2 CUPS | Calories: 199 | Protein: <1 gram | Carbohydrates: <1 gram | Fiber: 0 grams | Fat: 22 grams | Sodium: 14 milligrams

2 egg yolks

2 teaspoons lemon juice (or any variety of vinegar)

1 teaspoon mustard (optional, any style will work)

1 cup olive oil (or walnut or almond oil)

1. Combine egg yolks, lemon juice, and mustard in a food processor bowl. Pulse 10 times to combine well.

2. Stream in the oil while the processor is running until mixture thickens, or emulsifies.

3. Remove the mixture to a reusable container and refrigerate for up to 30 days.

GF PANKO-STYLE BREAD CRUMBS

MAKES 4 CUPS | Calories: 107 | Protein: 2 grams | Carbohydrates: 24 grams | Fiber: <1 gram | Fat: <1 gram | Sodium: 383 milligrams

8 cups white rice puffs (certified GF)

½ teaspoon sea salt

1. Place ingredients in a zip-top bag. With a rolling pin, roll the rice puff mixture until crushed into crumbs.

2. Transfer the crumbs to a reusable container and store for up to 2 months.

GF HOMEMADE VEGETABLE STOCK

MAKES 2 QUARTS | Calories: 10 | Protein: 0 grams | Carbohydrates: 3 grams | Fiber: 0 grams | Fat: 0 grams | Sodium: 54 milligrams

1 cup green onions (cut into 3" slices)

1 large yellow onion (peeled and cut into quarters; use Maui or Vidalia onion for extra sweetness)

2 celery stalks

2 carrots (cut into 3"-long pieces)

6 sprigs fresh thyme

8 sprigs fresh parsley

2 bay leaves

1 garlic clove

2 teaspoons sea salt

1 teaspoon black pepper

2 quarts cold water, or as needed to cover

1. Heat a large soup pot, or saucepan, to medium-high heat.

2. Add all ingredients to the pot and cover with the cold water. Bring mixture to a boil and then lower the heat to a simmer. Simmer for 4 hours, remove the thyme and bay leaves, and purée the mixture with your hand blender.

3. Use the stock immediately or cool and freeze in a container for future use.

GF HOMEMADE CHICKEN STOCK

MAKES 2 QUARTS | Calories: 15 | Protein: 1 gram | Carbohydrates: 4 grams | Fiber: 0 grams | Fat: 0 grams | Sodium: 64 milligrams

1 pound fresh whole chicken (cut into 5 pieces)

1 large yellow onion (peeled and cut into quarters; use Maui or Vidalia onion for extra sweetness)

2 celery stalks

2 carrots (cut into 3"-long pieces)

5 fresh thyme sprigs

7 fresh parsley sprigs

7 fresh dill sprigs

1 head of garlic (cut off top to expose top of cloves)

2 teaspoons sea salt

1 teaspoon white pepper (optional)

Cold water as needed to cover

1. Heat a large soup pot, or saucepan, to medium-high heat.

2. Add all ingredients to the pot and cover with cold water. Bring mixture to a boil and then lower the heat to a simmer. Simmer for 4 hours, remove the chicken and as many vegetables as possible, and strain the liquid back into the soup pot to remove the herbs.

3. Use the stock immediately or cool and freeze in a container for future use.

GF CORNMEAL PIZZA CRUST

MAKES 1 CRUST | Calories: 254 | Protein: 8 grams | Carbohydrates: 32 grams | Fiber: 5 grams | Fat: 10 grams | Sodium: 313 milligrams

1¾ cups warm water

1 tablespoon GF yeast

2 eggs

1 teaspoon sea salt

4 tablespoons olive oil

1 cup GF garbanzo/fava flour

1 cup cornmeal

1. Preheat oven to 425°F.

2. In a large bowl, combine water and yeast. Let stand a few minutes.

3. Add eggs, salt, and oil to mixture and blend briefly.

4. Add flour and cornmeal to food processor and blend about a minute on medium speed, until combined.

5. Leave dough in bowl, split in half, cover with plastic wrap, and allow to rise 20 minutes.

6. Place dough on greased pizza pan and, using wet hands, spread out dough to cover the full pan.

7. Bake without topping for 7–9 minutes.

GET THE **EDGE**

To make this recipe without using eggs, combine 2 tablespoons flaxseed meal and 6 tablespoons water; let stand one minute. Add to recipe as you would the eggs.

CARLY'S TOMATO SAUCE

MAKES 2 CUPS | Calories: 79 | Protein: 1 gram | Carbohydrates: 9 grams | Fiber: 2 grams | Fat: 5 grams | Sodium: 220 milligrams

2 tablespoons olive oil (use the best you have)

1 medium yellow onion (chopped fine)

1 green pepper (seeds removed, chopped fine)

2 carrots (chopped fine)

2 celery stalks (chopped fine)

2 tablespoons tomato paste

4 garlic cloves (minced fine)

¼ cup fresh basil (chopped)

2 tablespoons oregano (dried)

1 tablespoon raw brown sugar

1 28-ounce can San Marzano peeled tomatoes

2 tablespoons unsalted butter

1. Heat a medium saucepan to medium heat.

2. Add the oil, onions, peppers, carrots, celery, and tomato paste to the pan and stir until well combined.

3. Add the garlic, basil, oregano, sugar, and tomatoes to the vegetable mixture and stir well.

4. Add the butter and salt and pepper and stir the mixture well. Cover and simmer, on low heat, for 45 minutes.

5. Let the sauce cool and store in a reusable container.

BASIC AIOLI (FRENCH OR ITALIAN MAYONNAISE)

MAKES 1½ CUPS | Calories: 170 | Protein: 1 gram | Carbohydrates: <1 gram | Fiber: 0 grams | Fat: 18 grams | Sodium: 65 milligrams

2 eggs at room temperature

2 cloves garlic

1 teaspoon gluten-free English mustard

1 tablespoon fresh lemon juice or white wine vinegar

½ cup olive oil

½ cup canola oil

Salt and pepper to taste

1. Place the eggs, garlic, mustard, and lemon juice or vinegar in the bowl of your food processor. Blend vigorously.

2. Pulse and very slowly add the oils, salt, and pepper. Refrigerate in a closed container. (Some variations you can try include adding ½ teaspoon anchovy paste, or to taste; lemon zest; various herbs; coriander seed; anise seed; chili sauce; or chopped fresh fennel.)

GET THE **EDGE**

Aioli and mayonnaise are made with basically the same ingredients, with one exception: Aioli has a good lot of garlic flavor in it. It is loaded with character and can be spooned into Mediterranean seafood stews and soups or spread on gluten-free bread and sprinkled with cheese for a tasty crouton. Drop spoonfuls in soups or serve with seafood as a dressing.

FRESH GLUTEN-FREE CROUTONS

MAKES 24 CROUTONS | Calories: 200 | Protein: 1 gram | Carbohydrates: 8 grams | Fiber: <1 gram | Fat: 18 grams | Sodium: 269 milligrams

½ cup olive oil

Canola oil spray

2 cloves garlic, minced or put through a garlic press

4 slices gluten-free bread, thickly cut, crusts removed

Salt and pepper to taste

1. Preheat the broiler to 550°F.

2. Mix the oil and garlic. Brush both sides of the bread with the mixture. Sprinkle with salt and pepper.

3. Cut each slice of bread into 6 cubes, to make 24 cubes. Spray a cookie sheet with nonstick spray. Place the cubes on the sheet and broil until well browned on both sides.

4. Put the cookie sheet on the bottom rack of the oven. Turn off the oven and leave the croutons to dry for 20 minutes.

5. Store in an airtight container until ready to use.

GET THE **EDGE**

Garlic will give you various degrees of potency depending on how you cut it. Finely minced garlic, or that which has been put through a press, will be the strongest. When garlic is sliced, it is less strong, and when you leave the cloves whole, they are even milder.

INCREDIBLE HOLLANDAISE SAUCE

MAKES 1¼ CUPS | Calories: 186 | Protein: <1 gram | Carbohydrates: 0 grams | Fiber: 0 grams | Fat: 20 grams | Sodium: 129 milligrams

2 sticks (1 cup) unsalted butter

1 whole egg and 1 or 2 egg yolks, depending on the richness desired

1 tablespoon freshly squeezed lemon juice

⅛ teaspoon cayenne pepper

Salt to taste

1. Melt the butter in a small, heavy saucepan over very low heat.
2. Put the eggs, lemon juice, and cayenne in the jar of a blender or food processor. Blend well.
3. With the motor running on low, add the hot butter, a little at a time, to the egg mixture.
4. Return mixture to the pan you used to melt the butter. Whisking constantly, thicken the sauce over low heat, adding salt. As soon as it is thick, pour into a bowl, a sauce boat, or over the food. (Heating the sauce to thicken it is the delicate stage. You must not let it get too hot or it will scramble the eggs, or even curdle them. If either happens, add a tablespoon of boiling water and whisk vigorously.)

GET THE **EDGE**

The name implies that this sauce was devised in Holland, a land of high butter use. However, it is not called Holland sauce; we get a French spelling. In any area where there is plentiful butter, hollandaise sauce, with its rich, smooth texture, will reign. And although people tend to think of it in terms of eggs Benedict, it's good on most green vegetables.

GF CREPES

MAKES 8 | Calories: 327 | Protein: 16 grams | Carbohydrates: 36 grams | Fiber: 9 grams | Fat: 13 grams | Sodium: 227 milligrams

1¼ cups Rice Dream or soy milk

2 tablespoons unsalted butter

1 cup garbanzo/fava flour (sifted)

Pinch of salt

2 eggs

Canola oil spray

1. Warm the milk in a small saucepan with the butter over low heat. Continue heating until the butter is melted and then let cool for 3 minutes.

2. Add flour and salt to food processor and blend together. Add milk and butter mixture to flour while processor is running.

3. Add eggs to the food processor bowl to complete the batter and let rest for 30 minutes.

4. Spray a 7" crepe pan or 8" nonstick sauté pan with canola spray. Heat over medium-high heat until the pan is about to start smoking. Pour in ¼ cup of batter and cover the pan evenly.

5. Cook the crepe 3 minutes and flip over for another 2 minutes.

6. Remove crepe onto a plate covered with paper towels and respray pan. Repeat the process to make a total of 8 crepes. You can either refrigerate or freeze any crepes that you don't use immediately.

DESSERTS

Desserts are often hard to come by if you're living a gluten-free lifestyle, but in this section you will find a variety of desserts to match any meal. As you look through the recipes, you'll notice none of them contain refined sugar—everything is sweetened with natural sugars. You will also find recipes that include a soy-based, nondairy ice cream that everybody loves, especially those of you who are lactose intolerant.

DESSERTS CONTENTS

ORANGE AND RASPBERRY GRANITA

SERVES 4 | Calories: 147 | Protein: 2 grams | Carbohydrates: 34 grams | Fiber: 4 grams | Fat: <1 gram | Sodium: 4 milligrams

2 large navel oranges (¼" off top, slice off bottom)

1 cup fresh raspberries

2 tablespoons Gran Marnier orange liqueur

16 ounces orange juice

3 tablespoons raw brown sugar

GET THE **EDGE**

This recipe calls for raw sugar instead of refined sugar. Raw sugar tends to retain the minerals that existed prior to processing. Refined sugar loses much of its mineral content due to the refining process.

1. Remove the fruit of the oranges, being careful not to damage the orange skin. Place the orange skin in the freezer until solid.

2. Combine orange meat, raspberries, juice, sugar, and Gran Marnier in a strainer. With a spatula, press the fruit, liqueur, orange juice, and sugar through the strainer into a baking dish and stir. Place dish in freezer for 1 hour.

3. Remove baking dish from the freezer and, with 2 forks, scrape the "granita" in the dish. Spoon into the frozen orange skin and serve.

GF DOUBLE CHOCOLATE CHIP COOKIES

SERVES 4 | Calories: 297 | Protein: 2 grams | Carbohydrates: 35 grams | Fiber: 2 grams | Fat: 15 grams | Sodium: 158 milligrams

2¼ cups GF all-purpose baking flour

½ teaspoon baking powder

1 teaspoon baking soda

½ teaspoon salt

¼ teaspoon xanthan gum

¾ cup soy butter

¾ cup brown sugar (raw)

½ cup dark chocolate (raw, unsweetened)

2 eggs

2 teaspoons GF vanilla extract

2 cups GF semisweet chocolate chunks or chips

1. Preheat oven to 375°F.
2. Combine flour, baking powder, baking soda, salt, and xanthan gum in food processor bowl. Pulse ten times in the food processor. Remove to medium mixing bowl and set aside.
3. Combine butter, brown sugar, and raw chocolate in food processor bowl. Blend until creamy. Add eggs and vanilla and continue blending until well mixed. Gradually add the flour mixture until well mixed, then remove mixture from processor to mixing bowl and stir in chocolate chips.
4. Drop dough onto nonstick cookie sheets by rounded tablespoonfuls, 2 inches apart.
5. Bake for 9–12 minutes or until light golden brown. (DO NOT OVERBAKE.) Let stand 1–2 minutes and serve.

BERRIES WITH GRAN MARNIER WHIPPED CREAM

SERVES 4 | Calories: 118 | Protein: 2 grams | Carbohydrates: 21 grams | Fiber: 6 grams | Fat: 3 grams | Sodium: 44 milligrams

2 cups dairy-free whipped cream

2 tablespoons Gran Marnier orange liqueur

1 cup fresh blueberries

1 cup fresh raspberries

1 cup fresh strawberries

1 cup fresh blackberries

4 fresh mint sprigs

1. In a small mixing bowl add the whipped cream and liqueur and whisk to combine for 20 seconds.

2. Divide the berries among 4 dessert serving glasses and top with the whisked cream.

3. Garnish each with a mint sprig and serve.

GET THE **EDGE**

The berries in this recipe are refreshing and high in nutritional value, which is great for an occasional treat when you are trying to lose weight. Berries are sweet and easy to prepare and they are loaded with bioflavonoids, which can help to prevent cancer by retarding the growth of malignant cells.

WHITE POLKA DOT CHOCOLATE BROWNIES

SERVES 4 | Calories: 528 | Protein: 5 grams | Carbohydrates: 40 grams | Fiber: 2 grams |
Fat: 41 grams | Sodium: 443 milligrams

Canola oil spray

6 eggs

1 cup raw brown sugar

2 tablespoons vanilla extract

4 ounces raw white chocolate chunks

12 ounces GF semisweet chocolate mini-morsels

1 pound (4 sticks) soy butter

1 cup GF all-purpose baking flour

1 teaspoon salt

½ teaspoon xanthan gum

1. Preheat oven to 350°F.

2. Spray a 12" x 18" Pyrex baking dish with canola oil and set aside.

3. In large mixing bowl, mix eggs, sugar, and vanilla extract.

4. In a double boiler, melt half the chocolate morsels, and the butter, then add to the egg and sugar mixture.

5. Sift together the gluten-free flour, salt, and xanthan gum and stir into the chocolate mixture.

6. Stir in the remaining chocolate morsels. Spoon the mixture into the prepared pan and place white chocolate chunks every 2 inches on top of mixture. Bake for 30 minutes. Cool, cut into squares, and serve.

MANDARIN ORANGE AND CHOCOLATE CREPES

SERVES 4 | Calories: 741 | Protein: 17 grams | Carbohydrates: 78 grams | Fiber: 15 grams |
Fat: 41 grams | Sodium: 172 milligrams

1¼ cups Rice Dream or soy milk

2 tablespoons unsalted butter

1 cup garbanzo/fava flour (sifted)

¼ teaspoon salt

2 eggs

1 tablespoon Gran Marnier liqueur

Canola oil spray

12 ounces raw dark chocolate or carob plus
4 ounces shaved for garnish

Confectioners' sugar for garnish

2 16-ounce cans mandarin oranges
(drained)

½ cup orange zest

CREPES:

1. Warm the milk and butter in a small sauce-pan over low heat. Continue heating until the butter is melted, then remove from heat and then let cool for 3 minutes.

2. Add flour and salt to food processor and blend together. Add milk and butter mixture to flour while processor is running.

3. Add eggs and Gran Marnier to complete the batter and let rest for 30 minutes.

4. Spray a 7" crepe pan or 8" nonstick sauté pan with canola spray. Heat over medium-high heat until the pan is about to start smoking. Pour in ¼ cup of batter and cover the pan evenly. Cook the crepe 3 minutes, then flip over and cook for another 2 minutes.

5. Remove crepe onto a plate covered with paper towels and respray pan. Repeat process until 8 crepes are made.

FILLING:

1. Melt chocolate in a small saucepan over medium heat.

2. Place crepe on plate dusted with confectioners' sugar. Add 6 mandarin oranges to lower part of the crepe and pour melted chocolate over oranges to cover.

3. Roll crepe and sprinkle with orange zest and chocolate shavings then serve immediately.

CRISPY RICE MARSHMALLOW TREATS

SERVES 4 | Calories: 131 | Protein: 1 gram | Carbohydrates: 25 grams | Fiber: <1 gram | Fat: 3 grams | Sodium: 132 milligrams

3 tablespoons unsalted butter or soy butter

4 cups mini GF marshmallows

6 cups crispy rice puffs

Canola oil spray

1. Heat a large sauté pan to medium-high heat and melt the butter. Add marshmallows and cook until they are completely melted.

2. Add the crispy rice; stir. Spray a 13" x 9" Pyrex dish with canola oil and then transfer crispy rice mixture to the dish and spread out evenly. Let cool, cut into 2"-wide bars, and serve.

APPLE CIDER SORBET

SERVES 4 | Calories: 160 | Protein: <1 gram | Carbohydrates: 41 grams | Fiber: 1 gram | Fat: <1 gram | Sodium: 8 milligrams

2 cups fresh apple cider

2 large Red Delicious or Gala apples (peeled, cored, chopped medium)

4 tablespoons raw sugar

1 tablespoon lemon juice

½ tablespoon cinnamon (ground)

½ teaspoon nutmeg (grated fresh)

1. Heat a medium saucepan to medium-high heat. Add all ingredients to the pan and bring to a boil. Reduce heat to low and simmer about 10 minutes or until the apples are soft.

2. With a hand blender, purée the apple mixture until smooth, then remove to a freezer-safe vessel. Chill for 2 hours, stirring every 45 minutes, until frozen. Serve.

BANANA AND TOASTED COCONUT RICE PUDDING

SERVES 4 | Calories: 286 | Protein: 7 grams | Carbohydrates: 43 grams | Fiber: 2 grams | Fat: 9 grams | Sodium: 147 milligrams

3 cups soy milk (vanilla optional)

4 egg whites (beaten)

2 eggs (beaten)

1 tablespoon GF vanilla extract

1 tablespoon dark rum

1 cup raw sugar

Pinch of salt

1 cup coconut (shredded)

1 cup white basmati rice (cooked)

2 ripe bananas (peeled, chopped small)

2 cups soy cream

1. Heat a medium-sized pot to medium heat. Add the milk, egg whites, eggs, vanilla, rum, sugar, and salt, and whisk together rapidly. Heat the mixture until it begins to steam. Then reduce the heat to low, add the soy cream, cover the pan, and cook for 50 minutes to an hour or until it thickens.

2. Meanwhile, heat a small sauté pan to medium-high heat. Add the raw coconut and toast it in the pan until lightly browned. Set aside.

3. Add the rice to the milk mixture in the pot. With a wooden spoon, blend the mixture together. Add the bananas and combine well.

4. Spoon the mixture into 4 bowls, top each bowl with a generous amount of toasted coconut, and serve.

GET THE **EDGE**

When you feel like you're craving something sweet for dessert, make sure that it is actually sweetness you are looking for. Many people think that they need something sweet when what their body actually wants is more protein. If you select this recipe for dessert, pair it with a light entrée because it is quite filling.

BLUEBERRY AND STRAWBERRY CRISP

SERVES 4 | Calories: 384 | Protein: 9 grams | Carbohydrates: 60 grams | Fiber: 9 grams | Fat: 14 grams | Sodium: 94 milligrams

Canola oil spray

4 teaspoons soy butter

½ cup raw brown sugar

⅓ cup garbanzo flour

¾ cup GF oatmeal

2 cups blueberries

2 cups strawberries (topped and cut in half)

2 teaspoons grape juice

4 tablespoons water

1. Preheat oven to 375°F. Spray an 8" square Pyrex baking dish with oil and set aside.

2. In a medium-size mixing bowl add the butter and sugar. With a whisk, blend the ingredients well.

3. Add the flour and oatmeal to the bowl and blend well. In a separate small mixing bowl, add the berries, juice, and water and stir well with a wooden spoon.

4. Pile the oatmeal mixture on top of the berries evenly and place the dish in the oven. Bake for 35–40 minutes or until golden brown. Let cool for 3 minutes and serve.

CAROB AND CHESTNUT TARTS

SERVES 4 | Calories: 535 | Protein: 4 grams | Carbohydrates: 60 grams | Fiber: 2 grams |
Fat: 31 grams | Sodium: 41 milligrams

1 cup tapioca flour

½ cup chestnut flour (plus a small amount for rolling out dough)

1½ sticks unsalted butter (cut into ½" cubes)

2 tablespoons raw sugar

4 tablespoons ice water

1 cup chestnuts (shelled, rough chopped)

1 cup carob (chopped small or small chips)

1. Preheat oven to 400°F.

2. In your food processor add both flours and butter. Pulse until small pea-size pieces form in the bowl, then remove contents to a medium-size mixing bowl and stir in the sugar and the ice water. Fold the dough over itself a few times, form it into a ball, and refrigerate for 30 minutes.

3. Once the dough is chilled, place it on a chestnut-floured hard surface and roll out flat to ¼" thickness.

4. Using a 3" ring cutter or sturdy drinking glass, cut the dough into 4 disks. Place the disks in an oil-sprayed muffin tin or individual tart cups and press gently around the middle of the disks to form a cup.

5. Place a tablespoon of chestnuts in each tart cup and top with a tablespoon of carob.

6. Bake for 20–25 minutes. Remove from the oven and serve.

CAROB-COATED MASCARPONE AND HONEY FILLED FIGS

SERVES 4 | Calories: 485 | Protein: 10 grams | Carbohydrates: 64 grams | Fiber: 5 grams | Fat: 22 grams | Sodium: 97 milligrams

2 cups water

2 tablespoons lemon juice

1 cinnamon stick

8 large dried Mission figs

1 cup carob chips

1 cup mascarpone cheese

4 tablespoons honey

1 tablespoon lemon zest

1. Heat a medium-size saucepan to medium-high heat. Add the water, lemon juice, and cinnamon stick and bring to a boil. Reduce the heat to low and continue cooking for 10 minutes.

2. Add the figs to the pan, then remove pan from heat, and cover. Let the figs absorb the moisture of the lemon-cinnamon liquid for 30 minutes.

3. Meanwhile, heat a medium saucepan to medium-high heat and fill it ⅔ full with water. Place the carob chips in a small saucepan and place it inside the medium saucepan to act as a double boiler to melt the carob chips. Once the chips are completely melted, reduce the heat to medium-low to keep the carob in a melted state.

4. In a small mixing bowl, add the cheese, honey, and zest and blend well with a spoon for about 20 seconds. Set aside.

5. Once the figs have absorbed all the liquid, remove ¼" of the top of each fig with a sharp paring knife.

6. With a chopstick, make a cavity in the middle of each fig and fill it with the cheese mixture.

7. Proceed to coat the figs with carob, placing each on a metal spoon and dunking it into the melted carob. Place on a large serving plate, and serve.

CHERRIES AND GREEN TEA YOGURT CAROB CUPS

SERVES 4 | Calories: 576 | Protein: 10 grams | Carbohydrates: 54 grams | Fiber: 4 grams | Fat: 29 grams | Sodium: 136 milligrams

2 cups carob chips

8 3-ounce paper cups

1 6-ounce tub low-fat vanilla yogurt

4 green tea bags (empty tea into a small bowl and discard bags)

1½ cups fresh Bing or Queen Anne cherries (rinsed, pitted, stemmed, rough chopped); save 8 whole cherries for garnish

1. Microwave carob chips on medium heat for 1 minute. Stir the chips to evenly mix the melting carob. Continue to microwave on medium for 20 seconds at a time and then stir. Continue this process until the carob is all melted.

2. With a small spatula, butter knife, or cooking brush, coat each upside down cup evenly with the melted carob and place them on a tray into your refrigerator.

3. Let cups chill for 20 minutes, then remove them from the refrigerator. Gently separate carob from the paper cups, and place carob cups upright on a large serving plate.

4. In a medium mixing bowl, add the yogurt and green tea and combine well.

5. Add chopped cherries and gently fold into the yogurt. Using a tablespoon, fill each cup with the yogurt mixture, top with a whole cherry, and serve.

DRE'S "BAVARIAN CREAM" FRUIT PARFAIT

SERVES 4 | Calories: 214 | Protein: 3 grams | Carbohydrates: 40 grams | Fiber: 3 grams | Fat: 6 grams | Sodium: 135 milligrams

1 8-ounce package strawberry gelatin

1 cup hot water (110°F)

1 ripe mango (peeled, pitted)

1 cup soy cream

1 cup fresh strawberries (washed, topped, chopped small, then refrigerated)

2 ripe kiwi fruits (peeled, chopped small, refrigerated)

4 mint sprigs (for garnish)

1. Combine the gelatin and the hot water in a medium-size mixing bowl. Stir until all of the gelatin is dissolved. Place the bowl in the refrigerator and let the gelatin set for about an hour.

2. Meanwhile, place the mango in a small mixing bowl and purée with a hand blender. Cover the mango purée with plastic wrap and refrigerate.

3. When the gelatin is set, add the cream to the bowl and stir gently for 20 seconds with a large metal spoon to combine well.

4. Add a tablespoon of mango purée to the bottom of a parfait glass. Then add a 2"-thick layer of the gelatin cream. Next, add 2 tablespoons of strawberries and another 2" layer of gelatin cream. Next, add 2 tablespoons of kiwi. Finish the parfait with another layer of gelatin cream. Repeat the process for a total of 4 parfaits, top each with a mint sprig, and serve.

FAST RASPBERRY AND CASSIS TAPIOCA PUDDING

SERVES 4 | Calories: 154 | Protein: 2 grams | Carbohydrates: 30 grams | Fiber: 3 grams | Fat: 1 gram | Sodium: 19 milligrams

1 cup soy milk (vanilla)

⅓ cup raw sugar

1 egg (beaten)

3 tablespoons Minute Tapioca

1 whole vanilla bean (tiny beans removed by splitting the pod and scraping them out; reserve the beans)

1 teaspoon vanilla extract

1½ cups fresh raspberries (rinsed, drained well)

4 tablespoons cassis liqueur

4 mint sprigs for garnish

1. Heat a medium saucepan to medium-high heat and add the milk, sugar, egg, tapioca, and vanilla beans while whisking rapidly. Bring to a boil while stirring constantly, remove from the heat, stir in the vanilla extract, and let stand for five minutes.

2. Evenly spoon the mixture into 4 parfait or sturdy glasses of your choice. Let cool in the refrigerator for 20–30 minutes or until well set.

3. Divide the raspberries evenly into the 4 glasses and gently combine them into the pudding.

4. Add a tablespoon of cassis over the top of each and gently stir it just once into the pudding. Top the pudding with a sprig of mint and serve.

GLUTEN-FREE TIRAMISU

SERVES 4 | Calories: 459 | Protein: 10 grams | Carbohydrates: 52 grams | Fiber: 2 grams | Fat: 23 grams | Sodium: 120 milligrams

½ cup soy ricotta cheese

2 tablespoons raw sugar

½ tablespoon vanilla extract

1 teaspoon cinnamon (ground)

8 GF lady fingers (cut in half lengthwise)

1 cup espresso/French roast coffee (brewed, room temperature)

1 cup carob chips

1. In a medium mixing bowl, add the cheese, sugar, vanilla, and cinnamon. Stir vigorously to combine the ingredients and chill in the refrigerator for 20 minutes.

2. Lay out the pre-split bottom and top halves of the lady fingers on a large serving plate. With a tablespoon, spoon a generous amount of coffee on both halves of each.

3. With a butter knife or small bladed spatula, spread a generous amount of the cheese mixture on the lady finger bottom halves and cover with the lady finger tops.

4. Microwave carob chips for 1 minute on the medium setting. Stir to check the melting process. Continue to heat the carob chips for 20 seconds at a time on medium until they are completely melted. Drizzle the melted carob over the lady fingers and serve.

PINEAPPLE COCONUT CAROB POPS

SERVES 4 | Calories: 637 | Protein: 8 grams | Carbohydrates: 67 grams | Fiber: 7 grams | Fat: 38 grams | Sodium: 102 milligrams

1 fresh pineapple (trimmed, cored, cut into 2" chunks)

8 ounces fresh pineapple juice

4 frozen pop molds or 4-ounce paper cups

4 frozen pop sticks

2 cups carob chips

2 cups shredded coconut

1. In your food processor add the pineapple chunks and juice. Pulse the pineapple mixture for about 10 pulses (the fruit should still be visible). Pour the pineapple mixture into the molds or cups, add the sticks, and freeze until solid or 1 hour.

2. Fill a medium-size saucepan ⅔ full of water and heat until it comes to a boil. In a small saucepan add the carob chips and place over the medium pan. Heat the carob until it melts and reduce the heat to low to keep the carob barely melted.

3. Heat a small sauté pan to medium heat and add the coconut. Toast the coconut until it just begins to turn light brown. Remove from the pan onto a medium-sized plate.

4. Unmold a pineapple pop and roll it into the barely melted carob and then immediately in the cooled coconut to coat. Serve immediately or freeze until ready to serve.

PISTACHIO AND DATE TOFUTTI FROZEN DESSERT

SERVES 4 | Calories: 558 | Protein: 13 grams | Carbohydrates: 90 grams | Fiber: 6 grams | Fat: 18 grams | Sodium: 34 milligrams

2 pints vanilla Tofutti or GF ice cream (set out for 5 minutes to be pliable)

1 cup fresh Medjool dates (chopped medium fine)

1 tablespoon fresh cinnamon (ground)

1 teaspoon fresh nutmeg (grated)

1 cup unsalted GF certified pistachio nuts (chopped medium fine)

½ cup honey

1. In a medium mixing bowl add the pliant Tofutti, dates, cinnamon, and nutmeg. Dip a large metal spoon in water and use the wet spoon to stir the mixture, combining it well.

2. Divide the mixture evenly into four 4" ramekins. Sprinkle a generous amount of pistachios over the top of each ramekin.

3. Drizzle a generous amount of honey over the top of the nuts and freeze for 15 minutes to chill. Remove from the freezer and serve.

POLENTA-CRUSTED FRESH PEACH TARTS

SERVES 4 | Calories: 319 | Protein: 1 gram | Carbohydrates: 42 grams | Fiber: 2 grams | Fat: 15 grams | Sodium: 117 milligrams

4 tablespoons unsalted butter

1 18-ounce package plain premade polenta

½ cup water

½ cup raw brown sugar

2 fresh yellow or white peaches (pitted, skinned, chopped medium)

1 cup soy cream

1. Preheat oven to 400°F.

2. Generously grease 4 cups in a muffin pan with butter.

3. Cut four 2"-wide slices of polenta and put each one in a greased cup in the mold pan. With a spoon, scoop out the center of each polenta slice, leaving about ¼ on the bottom of each slice, and press the sides against the mold to form a cup.

4. Melt a tablespoon of butter for each polenta slice and coat the inside of the polenta cup with the butter. Repeat this process with each polenta slice and place the pan in the oven. Bake the polenta for 10–12 minutes or until the cups just begin to brown. Remove from the oven and let cool.

5. Heat a small saucepan to medium-high heat. Add the water and sugar, then bring to a boil. Reduce the heat and cook until the mixture begins to thicken and then remove from the heat.

6. In a small mixing bowl coat ½ the peaches with sugar, then combine remaining peaches with the cream. Gently blend and place a spoonful into each polenta cup.

7. Spoon the other sugar-coated peaches on top and serve.

RASPBERRY ORANGE SHERBET WITH DARK CHOCOLATE BITS

SERVES 4 | Calories: 300 | Protein: 3 grams | Carbohydrates: 37 grams | Fiber: 4 grams | Fat: 15 grams | Sodium: 33 milligrams

¼ cup water (chilled)

1 teaspoon GF gelatin

¾ cup boiling water

¾ cup raw sugar, plus 3 tablespoons

2 tablespoons orange zest

¾ cup 100% orange juice

1 cup fresh raspberries (rinsed, drained well, chopped small)

1 egg yolk

½ cup soy cream

1 egg white

1 cup raw dark chocolate (chopped small)

1. In a small mixing bowl, add the chilled water and the gelatin and let the gelatin soak for 5 minutes. In a medium mixing bowl, combine the boiling water, ¾ cup of sugar, and the softened gelatin. Stir until well mixed and gelatin has completely dissolved.

2. Add the orange zest and juice, raspberries, and egg yolk, and stir to combine well.

3. In a large metal bowl combine the soy cream and 3 tablespoons sugar and whisk until the mixture becomes whipped cream.

4. In a medium metal bowl whisk the egg white until completely whipped into stiff peaks, then add the white to the whipped cream bowl and whisk to combine well.

5. Add the chocolate bits to the mixture, spoon the mixture into 4 freezer-safe shallow dishes or ramekins, and place in your freezer. Make sure to stir the sherbet a couple of times during the first hour. Let freeze for a total of about 2½ hours and serve.

"SOUTHERN STYLE" GRILLED PEACHES À LA MODE

SERVES 4 | Calories: 331 | Protein: 8 grams | Carbohydrates: 62 grams | Fiber: 3 grams | Fat: 7 grams | Sodium: 226 milligrams

4 fresh white or yellow peaches (peeled, pitted, and halved)

½ half fresh lemon

2 cups gluten-free graham crackers (smashed small)

1 pint vanilla Tofutti frozen dessert

1 cup fresh mint (chopped small)

1. Heat your indoor or outdoor grill to medium heat. Cook peach halves for 3–4 minutes per side or until they have nice grill marks. Remove to a serving plate.

2. Sprinkle the cooked peaches lightly with lemon juice.

3. Pour ½ cup of graham cracker crumbs into the bottom of a serving bowl. Place two cooked peach halves over the cracker crumbs and top with a generous ball of the Tofutti "ice cream."

4. Repeat this process 3 more times, then sprinkle the top of the Tofutti generously with mint and serve.

GET THE EDGE

Grilling peaches releases the natural sugar in the peaches so it is not necessary to add sugar for additional sweetness. Most people rave about the grilled flavor.

HENRY B'S GF GINGER CAKES

SERVES 4 | Calories: 718 | Protein: 12 grams | Carbohydrates: 89 grams | Fiber: 9 grams | Fat: 37 grams | Sodium: 341 milligrams

1 cup canola oil

1 cup GF molasses

½ teaspoon salt

2 teaspoons ginger (ground)

½ teaspoon cloves (ground)

2½ cups garbanzo flour

1 teaspoon baking soda

4 tablespoons unsalted butter or soy butter

1 cup raw brown sugar (½ for cake, ½ for sauce)

2 eggs (beaten in separate bowl)

1 cup boiling brewed coffee

¾ cup raisins

1 teaspoon cinnamon (ground)

1. Preheat oven to 350°F.

2. Add oil and molasses to food processor bowl and pulse 10 times until mixed.

3. Add salt, ginger, cloves, flour, and baking soda to bowl and blend for 30 seconds or until completely mixed.

4. Add 2 tablespoons of the butter and sugar to the mixture and blend for 30 seconds. Continue by adding the eggs and blend for 30 seconds. Next add the coffee and blend for 30 seconds. With a spatula, gently fold in the raisins to the mixture.

5. Transfer mixture to a greased or oil-sprayed 9" x 12" baking pan. Bake for 30 minutes. Cut into 8 equal pieces and serve.

PAVLOVA WITH CHOCOLATE AND BANANAS

SERVES 6 | Calories: 594 | Protein: 6 grams | Carbohydrates: 74 grams | Fiber: 2 grams | Fat: 32 grams | Sodium: 115 milligrams

4 egg whites

1 teaspoon vinegar

½ cup sugar plus ⅓ cup

Canola oil spray

3 squares semisweet carob

½ cup unsalted butter

2 bananas, kept in the freezer for 20 minutes to firm

1 cup soy cream, whipped with 2 teaspoons confectioners' sugar

1. Preheat oven to 200°F.

2. Whip the egg whites until very stiff, and as they stiffen, add the vinegar and slowly add the ½ cup of sugar. Transfer this meringue mixture to a 9" glass pie pan that you've treated with nonstick spray.

3. Bake the meringue for 2 hours. Then, turn off the oven and crack the door. Let the meringue rest for another hour. It should become very crisp and lightly browned. Do not store it for later use if the weather is humid.

4. Melt the carob, butter, and ⅓ cup sugar. Cool until mixture is still liquid but at room temperature.

5. Peel and slice 1 banana into the meringue crust. Spoon half of the carob sauce over it. Add the other banana and the remaining sauce, and top with whipped cream.

PANNA COTTA

SERVES 6 | Calories: 184 | Protein: 3 grams | Carbohydrates: 33 grams | Fiber: <1 gram | Fat: 5 grams | Sodium: 139 milligrams

2 teaspoons water

2 teaspoons unflavored gelatin

1 cup soy cream

⅓ cup sugar, or to taste

2 cups low-fat buttermilk, well shaken

1 teaspoon vanilla

Canola oil spray

Fresh fruit of your choice

1. Mix the water and gelatin together and let rest until gelatin "blooms," about 5 minutes.

2. Stir the cream and sugar in a saucepan over moderate heat until sugar dissolves. Do not boil. Whisk in the gelatin and water mixture; cool to room temperature. Whisk in buttermilk and vanilla.

3. Prepare 6 6-ounce custard cups with non-stick spray. Divide the custard among the cups. Refrigerate for 6 hours or overnight.

4. Run a sharp knife around the edge of each cup. Invert the cups on chilled plates. Serve with fresh berries.

GET THE EDGE

Panna cotta, the Italian custard dessert, is basically a custard made with buttermilk. Flan is also a custard and may be made with fruit. Custard is traditionally made with eggs, milk, sugar, and flavoring. Simple and easy to digest, these custards are basics for adults and children.

CAROB-RASPBERRY SOUFFLÉ

SERVES 4 | Calories: 342 | Protein: 9 grams | Carbohydrates: 46 grams | Fiber: 2 grams | Fat: 12 grams | Sodium: 105 milligrams

2 squares carob

½ cup sugar

1 tablespoon butter plus 1 tablespoon for soufflé dish

2 tablespoons Chambord (raspberry liqueur)

3 tablespoons garbanzo flour or cornstarch

3 tablespoons cold soy milk

4 egg yolks

5 egg whites

Pinch cream of tartar

½ pint fresh raspberries, rinsed and allowed to dry on paper towels

1. Preheat the oven to 375°F.

2. In a medium-sized, heavy saucepan, melt the carob with the sugar, butter, and Chambord. Remove from heat. Whisk the flour and milk together and add to the carob mixture.

3. Beat the egg yolks, one at a time, into the carob mixture. Whip the egg whites and cream of tartar together until stiff. Fold the egg whites into the carob mixture and pour into a buttered 1½-quart soufflé dish.

4. Bake for 35–40 minutes or until puffed and brown. Top each portion with fresh raspberries and garnish with whipped soy cream if desired.

GET THE **EDGE**

The variety of soufflés you can make is limited only by the availability of ingredients and your imagination. You can substitute mashed bananas for the carob, or mangos, for that matter. The soufflé makes a marvelous presentation, but it must be served immediately.

PUMPKIN CUSTARD

SERVES 6 TO 8 | Calories: 277 | Protein: 6 grams | Carbohydrates: 44 grams | Fiber: 2 grams | Fat: 9 grams | Sodium: 105 milligrams

2 cups cubed fresh pumpkin, steamed in 1 cup water, or 2 (12–13 ounce) packages frozen winter squash, thawed

½ cup brown sugar

¼ cup white sugar

½ teaspoon each: ground ginger, ground cloves, ground nutmeg

1 teaspoon ground cinnamon

3 eggs, beaten

1 cup soy cream

1. Preheat oven to 325°F.

2. Purée the steamed pumpkin in your blender or food processor. Slowly add the rest of the ingredients.

3. Pour into a buttered 8" x 8" casserole dish. Place a roasting pan of hot water in the middle of the oven. Put the dish of pumpkin custard in the roasting pan and bake for 50–60 minutes. A nice variation is to add a cup of pecan pieces and let them bake right in the custard.

GET THE **EDGE**

You can substitute frozen winter (butternut) squash for the pumpkin with good results. Canned pumpkin is very heavy and strong— and may contain hidden gluten—so try to avoid it.

RICE PUDDING WITH APRICOTS

SERVES 6 TO 8 | Calories: 425 | Protein: 10 grams | Carbohydrates: 56 grams | Fiber: 4 grams | Fat: 19 grams | Sodium: 63 milligrams

1 cup dried apricots, cut into quarters

1 cup water

½ cup sugar

1 cup rice (basmati is preferable)

2½ cups soy milk

1 teaspoon vanilla

⅛ teaspoon nutmeg

½ cup sugar, or more to taste

1 cup soy cream, whipped stiff

8 ounces blanched almonds, toasted, for garnish

1. Bring the apricots, water, and sugar to a boil and turn down heat. Simmer until the apricots are plump and the sauce syrupy and remove from heat.

2. In a large, heavy pot, mix the rice and milk. Bring to a boil and then turn down heat to simmer. Cook for about 60 minutes, stirring occasionally.

3. Stir the vanilla, nutmeg, and sugar into the rice. Cool slightly. Fold the whipped cream into the rice mixture, and then fold in the apricots. Top with toasted almonds.

PART 3

The Seven-Day Weight-Loss Plan

ONE OF THE BIGGEST CHALLENGES for people struggling with their weight is maintaining their weight loss. Oftentimes, people diet, lose weight, and then gain it back over and over again. But this plan is different; it will help you get off the weight-loss roller coaster and keep those extra pounds off for good. Why? Because going gluten-free and eating healthy is not a "diet," it is a lifestyle change. Long-term weight control is not successful when you are required to weigh and measure foods, or count calories or fat grams—or when you are forced to deprive yourself of the foods you love. When you give up processed foods containing gluten, you don't have to count or measure, and you can still eat the gourmet foods that you love. The foods you eat will be healthy *and* gratifying.

But to lose weight, you also want to make sure that you're actually eating these healthy, gratifying foods. Many people skip meals because they think this will help them slim down, but this can lead to weight *gain*. When you miss a meal your metabolism responds by slowing down in an effort to conserve your energy. And, when weight loss happens too quickly—for example, if you severely restrict your calorie intake—your body thinks it is starving and will fight to survive by reserving fat stores. Most of the weight you'll lose under these circumstances is water weight, which you'll probably gain back. Instead, your focus should be on losing only body fat. Eating regular meals and snacks is the best way to lose weight, regulate blood sugar, enhance fat burning, and increase energy, so be prepared if you know that you will be away from home for a long time. Take healthy gluten-free snacks such as a bean salad or carrot chips with green pea hummus with you so you won't be tempted to eat junk food or fast food.

It is also important to pay attention to how your body feels when you eat (and you *know* you don't feel good when you splurge on junk food!). Put down your fork when you are satisfied and avoid emotional eating caused by stress, boredom, and fatigue. If you find yourself standing in front of the refrigerator with the door open, picking at leftovers because you are bored, try going for a long walk or bicycle ride instead. Talk to your health-care practitioner about an exercise program that will help you achieve your weight-loss goals.

Our seven-day gluten-free weight-loss program tells you how to use the delicious, nutrient-dense recipes found throughout the book—all of which include a healthy balance of lean proteins, complex carbohydrates, and unsaturated fats—to get the energy you need. Because you should eat frequently throughout the day to avoid dips in blood sugar that can result in fatigue, mood swings, and overeating at meals, we've included snacks. To be sure you stay on the program even if your days are hectic, prepare several recipes in advance and freeze them for a quick meal during the week.

So, get ready to live a healthy, gluten-free lifestyle. It's going to be delicious!

DAY ONE	
Glass of 100-percent juice or herbal tea upon awakening (if desired)	
BREAKFAST	Berry Omelet
LUNCH	Four-Bean Salad
SNACK	Carrot and celery sticks with store-bought hummus
DINNER	Grilled Shrimp Salad and Zucchini, Tomato, and Portobello Roulade
DESSERT	Pistachio and Date Frozen Dessert (if desired)

DAY TWO	
Glass of 100-percent juice or herbal tea upon awakening (if desired)	
BREAKFAST	Breakfast Parfait
LUNCH	Turkey and Cilantro Lettuce Wraps
SNACK	Raw vegetables or raw, unsalted nuts
DINNER	A generous portion of Lentils and Cabbage, plus tossed salad with any raw vegetables and avocado
DESSERT	Berries with Gran Marnier Whipped Cream

DAY THREE	
Glass of 100-percent juice or herbal tea upon awakening (if desired)	
BREAKFAST	Spiced Apple Oatmeal
LUNCH	Curried Bay Shrimp and Broccoli Salad
SNACK	Carrot Chips
DINNER	Poblano Chicken, Cauliflower "Mashed Potatoes," Roasted Artichoke and Vegetable Salad
DESSERT	None

DAY FOUR

Glass of 100-percent juice or herbal tea upon awakening (if desired)

BREAKFAST	Scrambled Eggs with Leeks and fresh fruit
LUNCH	Tomato Basil Soup and Toasted Sesame and Garlic Cauliflower Salad
SNACK	Choose any raw vegetables
DINNER	Zucchini Boats with King Crab, Grapefruit and Avocado Salad
DESSERT	Fresh berries (if desired)

DAY FIVE

Glass of 100-percent juice or herbal tea upon awakening (if desired)

BREAKFAST	Gluten-free oatmeal and fresh fruit
LUNCH	El Vaquero Chicken Salad
SNACK	Pineapple, Apple, and Mandarin Orange Yogurt Smoothie
DINNER	Vegetarian Spaghetti and "Meatballs," Curried Bay Shrimp and Broccoli Salad
DESSERT	Orange and Raspberry Granita

DAY SIX

Glass of 100-percent juice or herbal tea upon awakening (if desired)

BREAKFAST	Spinach and Bay Shrimp Omelet and fesh fruit
LUNCH	Eggplant Stack with Avocado, Hummus, and Roasted Pepper or large tossed salad with 1 can of white tuna packed in water and gluten-free dressing
SNACK	Raw, unsalted nuts and/or a few large raw carrots
DINNER	Grilled Halibut with Guacamole; Ratatouille; Grilled Portobello Mushroom, Red Onion, and Zucchini Salad
DESSERT	Fresh berries (if desired)

DAY SEVEN

Glass of 100-percent juice or herbal tea upon awakening (if desired)

BREAKFAST	Tofu Omelet with Spinach, Mushrooms, Parmesan Cheese, and Garlic
LUNCH	Chopped Roast Turkey Salad
SNACK	Fresh vegetables and/or beans
DINNER	Tofu with Vegetables and Thai Peanut Sauce, Sweet Potato Salad
DESSERT	None

ADDITIONAL WEIGHT-LOSS TIPS

1. Consult your doctor before beginning any weight-loss program.
2. Drink only water with meals and anytime during the day. Your kidneys need plenty of water to work properly. A lack of water can affect the productivity of your liver, which can result in stored fat.
3. Fruit and vegetable juice must be labeled "100-percent juice." Read labels to check for added sugar.
4. For best results, do not eat after 8:00 P.M. This is because most people are usually less active after dinner than they are during the day. Therefore, food eaten after 8:00 P.M. is more likely to be stored as fat. If you do need to eat late because of a social event, do some light activity before you go to sleep for the evening.
5. If you choose a recipe with animal protein for lunch, it is best to have a vegetarian meal for dinner and vice versa. This will help you to avoid boredom and provide you with a wide variety of nutrients in your day as well as varied sources of protein and carbohydrates.
6. Do not eat the same foods for breakfast, lunch, and dinner two days in a row. This is important to avoid boredom and to get a wide range of nutrients from eating a variety of foods. Snacks can be the same or varied.

GLUTEN-FREE LIBATIONS

You don't have to give up the drinks you love just because you're following a gluten-free diet. In fact, all distilled alcoholic beverages are gluten-free, including bourbon, vodka, scotch, and wine. Most beer does contain gluten, but there are companies that produce gluten-free beer. Be careful though. If libations have flavoring that is added after being distilled they may have been contaminated with gluten.

Wine

For the most part, all wine (including sake) is gluten-free, but you always want to check with the manufacturer to make sure its wine doesn't come into contact with anything that could compromise the product.

The following is a list of vintners whose wines we recommend:

- Benziger
- Beringer
- Clos Du Bois
- Copper Ridge
- Estancia
- Fenn Valley
- Five Oaks
- Francis Coppola
- Ingleside—Only the Blue Crab Blanc, Blue Crab Blush, Pinot Grigio, Sauvignon Blanc, Rosato de Sangiovese, Viognier, The Rose, and October Harvest are gluten-free
- J. Lohr
- Kendall Jackson
- La Rocca
- Ravenswood
- Robert Sinskey
- Stag's Leap

In addition to wines, you also want to watch out for wine coolers. Most contain barley malt and are not gluten-free.

Gluten-Free Ale and Beer

Most beer is made from barley, so it contains gluten. Fortunately, there are now several companies that make beer from buckwheat, sorghum, rice, or millet, which are all gluten-free. Here is a list of gluten-free options:

- Bard's Tale Beer
- Lake Front Brewery—New Grist is a winner of the G.F. Beer Festival
- O'Brien Brewery—Australia's first gluten-free beer is a winner of the G.F. Beer Festival
- Redbridge—Sorghum Beer by Anheuser Busch
- Ramapo Valley Brewery—Passover Honey Beer is a winner of the gluten-free Beer Festival

Vodka

All distilled vodka is gluten-free, but you should always check with the manufacturer to ensure that what you're drinking is okay. The vodkas in the following list are recommended:

1. Adamba
2. Blue Ice
3. Chopin
4. Ciroc—made from French grapes
5. Cold River Vodka
6. Jankill

Popular Party Drinks

You can still enjoy an occasional cocktail even though you are on a gluten-free diet. Always read the product label to check for gluten-containing ingredients. If you are still not sure that a product is gluten-free, check with the manufacturer. Following are some recipes for gluten-free cocktails.

GINGER RUM CHAMPAGNE PUNCH

5 QUARTS | Calories: 85 | Protein: 0 grams | Carbohydrates: 20 grams | Fiber: 0 grams | Fat: 0 grams | Sodium: 7 milligrams

1 (2-quart) bottle white grape juice made of 100-percent juice

1–2 liters ginger ale to taste

1 cup white rum

1 cup raspberries (optional)

1 cup blackberries (optional)

1 cup strawberries, cut in half with the green stem still attached (optional)

1 cup blueberries (optional)

1 cup orange slices

1. Place white grape juice and ginger ale in refrigerator overnight or until well chilled.

2. In a serving pitcher or punch bowl, pour equal parts white grape juice and ginger ale. Then add the rum. Stir gently. Fill each glass, and garnish with fruit.

GET THE **EDGE**

Placing fruit in the freezer for a couple of hours before serving will make your cocktails nice and icy.

PIÑA COLADA

SERVES 1 | Calories: 200 | Protein: 1 gram | Carbohydrates: 8 grams | Fiber: 0 grams | Fat: 4 grams | Sodium: 22 milligrams

2 ounces coconut rum

2 ounces pineapple juice

1 ounce cream

1. Blend all ingredients together with crushed ice and pour into a tall glass.

2. For a tropical feel, garnish with a slice of pineapple and an umbrella.

LONG ISLAND ICED TEA

SERVES 1 | Calories: 201 | Protein: 0 grams | Carbohydrates: 18 grams | Fiber: 0 grams | Fat: 0 grams | Sodium: 34 milligrams

½ ounce light rum

½ ounce gin

½ ounce vodka

½ ounce tequila

1 ounce sour mix

8 ounces cola

Lemon wedge (to garnish)

1. Pour the spirits and sour mix into a collins glass with ice.

2. Stir well or mix with a shaker then add cola and mix well.

3. Garnish with the lemon wedge.

COOKING MEASUREMENT EQUIVALENTS

THIS = THIS	
1 tablespoon	3 teaspoons
¹⁄₁₆ cup	1 tablespoon
⅛ cup	2 tablespoons
⅙ cup	2 tablespoons + 2 teaspoons
¼ cup	4 tablespoons
⅓ cup	5 tablespoons + 1 teaspoon
⅜ cup	6 tablespoons
½ cup	8 tablespoons
⅔ cup	10 tablespoons + 2 teaspoons
¾ cup	12 tablespoons
1 cup	48 teaspoons
1 cup	16 tablespoons
8 fluid ounces	1 cup
1 pint	2 cups
1 quart	2 pints
4 cups	1 quart
1 gallon	4 quarts
16 ounces	1 pound

INDEX

ABOUT THE AUTHORS

Gini Warner, MA, completed her master's degree in health education and nutritional science at New York University in 1988 and has been working with families, individuals, and corporations in the fields of weight loss, celiac disease, food intolerance, immune dysfunction, diabetes, osteoporosis, and overall wellness. She has been a clinical nutritionist for more than twenty years. Gini has developed wellness programs for corporations nationwide including AT&T, Citibank, and Revlon and writes articles for several online newsletters including *The Celiac Spru News*, *celiaccentral.org*, and *www.glutenfreeclub.com*. Gini has offices in Laguna Beach and Laguna Niguel, California, and lives in Laguna Beach, California. You can visit her online at *www.healthbygini.com*.

Chef Ross Harris began his culinary career as a chef at Hochman's Delicatessen in Newport Beach, California, in 1974, before moving on to work as assistant head chef at the Five Points Grille in Huntington Beach, California. There, Chef Ross became known for his ability to bake his own breads and roll his own pasta, giving his customers the choice of traditional or gluten-free ingredients. Before becoming a personal chef, he worked as the assistant head chef at Le Diplomat, an exclusive Mediterranean-cuisine restaurant in Southern California, where he cooked for illustrious gourmands and celebrities, including the Maloof family, Marlo Thomas, and George Lopez. He currently lives in Southern California.

Dr. Peter Green, MD (Foreword author), is the director of the Celiac Disease Center at Columbia University. He is a former president of the New York Society of Gastrointestinal Endoscopy and remains on the Council of the Society. He was on the Postgraduate Educational Committee, is a member of the American Society for Gastrointestinal Endoscopy, and is a founding member of the Clinical Teaching Project, a committee established by the American Gastroenterological Association to develop teaching materials for gastroenterologists.